A GRIZZLY TALE

A Father and Daughter Survival Story

Johan Otter

INDIE BOOKS INTERNATIONAL

Copyright © 2016 by Johan Otter.
All rights reserved.
Printed in the United States of America.

No part of this publication may be reproduced or distributed in any form or by any means without the prior permission of the publisher. Requests for permission should be directed to permissions@indiebooksintl.com, or mailed to Permissions, Indie Books International, 2424 Vista Way, Suite 316, Oceanside, CA 92054.

Neither the publisher nor the author is engaged in rendering legal or other professional services through this book. If expert assistance is required, the services of an appropriate professional should be sought. The publisher and the author shall have neither liability nor responsibility to any person or entity with respect to any loss or damage caused directly or indirectly by the information in this publication.

ISBN-10: 1-941870-64-3
ISBN-13: 978-1-941870-64-8
Library of Congress Control Number: 2016945831

Designed by Joni McPherson, www.mcphersongraphics.com

Photographs on page 115 and 123 are used with permission from the *Los Angeles Times*. All other photographs owned by Johan Otter.

Schaben, Allen J., photographer. *ANOTHER ORDEAL ENDS*. Photograph. Los Angeles: *Los Angeles Times*, April 30, 2007.

Schaben, Allen J., photographer. *Nearly a year after his attack, back on the Grinnell Glacier Trail in Glacier National Park, Montana*. Photograph. Los Angeles: *Los Angeles Times*, February 29, 2008.

INDIE BOOKS INTERNATIONAL, LLC
2424 VISTA WAY, SUITE 316
OCEANSIDE, CA 92054
www.indiebooksintl.com

— TABLE OF CONTENTS —

PROLOGUE 7

CHAPTER 1: August 25, 2005: Glacier National Park 13

CHAPTER 2: The Netherlands and the Stubbornness of the Dutch. 15

CHAPTER 3: An Immigrant's Story. 19

CHAPTER 4: A Family's Story 25

CHAPTER 5: Life Interrupted. 47

CHAPTER 6: The Rescue. 61

CHAPTER 7: Life, Reset 73

CHAPTER 8: The Road to Recovery: Seattle 91

CHAPTER 9: The Road to Recovery: San Diego 97

CHAPTER 10: Discharge: Going Home 103

CHAPTER 11: The New Normal 117

CHAPTER 12: Return to Glacier 127

POSTSCRIPT 137

ACKNOWLEDGMENTS 143

Grizzly bear next to the road in the Many Glacier area. This time I was inside my car.

These bears are much better looking from a safe distance than at arm's length away.

— PROLOGUE —

by Marilyn Otter

It is 6 p.m. on August 25 in Escondido, California, just north of San Diego. Although my birthday was yesterday, nothing eventful has occurred. That's because half of my family—my husband, Johan, and my eldest daughter, Jenna—is away on a two-week hiking trip though Wyoming and Montana. We'll do the birthday celebrating when they return, which makes more sense since Johan's birthday is on September 8. We'll just have one big shindig then. Besides, I am so bone tired right now that a party would be wasted on me. I am a tenth-grade English teacher, and my students have already been in school for fourteen days. The honeymoon period of easy review assignments is over and now the work begins. I cringe when I think of grading those soon-to-be-written essays.

The phone rings. Normally I would let it ring and listen to the message. This time I decide to answer, thinking it might be my daughter, Jenna, or my husband, Johan calling to wish me a happy birthday.

"Hello, Otter residence."

"Mrs. Otter?"

"Yes."

"This is Kalispell Emergency Room. I have Jenna with me, and she'd like to speak to you."

"…OK."

The hairs on the back of my neck awaken and I feel a slight tingling sensation down my spine.

"Mom?"

"Jenna?"

"Mom, dadandigotattackedbyagrizzlybearwhenwewerehiking!"

"[Pause] What? What do you mean?"

I think, "Yeah, right. What really happened? This is not funny!"

Jenna's voice, slightly calmer now, answers, "Dad and I were attacked by a grizzly while we were hiking."

How does one reply to this?

"Are you all right? Is Dad ok?"

"I'm cut up and bruised, but all right. Dad is being taken to another hospital, but he's doing OK. The nurse is going to talk to you now."

"OK, Jen."

I am very focused and methodical, perhaps in a bit of shock. A calm adult voice speaks.

"Mrs. Otter, I'm a nurse here in the emergency room at Kalispell Hospital in Montana. Johan wanted us to let Jenna talk to you first so you wouldn't be as worried. We tried to call you a couple of times earlier, but no one was home and we didn't want to leave a message for something like this.

"First of all, Jenna and Johan are safe and they're going to be all right. They were mauled by a grizzly bear. Jenna is doing well. Her wounds have been treated. She's going to need a short surgery to fix a tear in her shoulder.

"Johan had it worse, but he's going to be OK, too. His injuries require a transfer to Harborview General in Seattle. We're preparing him for helicopter transport right now. The doctors in Seattle have the facilities to treat his injuries, and they'll be waiting for him."

Stephanie, our younger daughter, who is 16, has wandered in from the other room. She doesn't hear the whole conversation, but senses something is off. After I hang up, she looks at me, quizzically.

"Steph, first of all, I don't want to panic you. Jenna and Dad are all *right,* [well, not really all right] *but they were attackedbyagrizzlybearwhentheywerehiking."*

Steph's wrinkled brows and tearing eyes show her fear and disbelief. "What do you mean?"

I finally notice her friend Kate is here, too. She is clearly concerned and looks ready to offer her help.

"I just talked to Jenna from the emergency room in Montana. She and dad got attacked by a grizzly bear in Glacier. I don't know much more. They are flying dad to Seattle. Jenna is staying in Kalispell to get treated there. I've got to go to Dad."

I really don't comprehend Steph's reply.

I phone Kate's mother, Laura. Meanwhile, Kate and Steph go upstairs, where they frantically rummage through my clothing drawers and closet to pack an overnight bag for me. (Later, when I am calmer, I can't help chuckling over some of the fashion statements they've selected—the tackiest, overstretched sweatshirt I own coupled with a pair of high water pants—much of it stuff I meant to throw out or give away).

Downstairs, I'm on the phone.

"Laura, Johan and Jenna were attackedbyagrizzlybearwhilehiking."

"What! Oh my god; oh my god! What do you need me to do for you?"

"I need a ride to the airport."

"Ok, Marilyn. Don't worry. I'm calling the airport right now to get you on a flight tonight. I'll get it. You can pay me later. You just get yourself ready. I'll call you back in a few minutes."

Maybe it's my automatic stress response, but I am amazingly calm as I methodically plan how to manage the situation. I phone my sister, and we arrange for my brother-in-law to connect with Jenna in Montana and pick up Johan's truck, which is still parked at the lodge in Glacier National Park. I call my sister and ask her to check in on Steph back home in Escondido. I've already decided Steph will stay with Kate and Laura during the school week so she can maintain some sense of normalcy.

Everything is moving like clockwork.

Laura has secured a 9:00 p.m. flight to Seattle for me. Stephanie and Kate have packed my overnight bag with the basic necessities—fashion be damned. By 7:50, all of us are on our way to the airport.

Sitting in the car allows me the first chance to get a grasp on my feelings. Bodily, I am in the van, but mentally I am in a state of free-floating anxiety. I do not feel the pressure of the seat, yet I am hyperaware of every air molecule brushing against the hair follicles of my arms. It's quiet in the car; none of us knows what to say.

Laura breaks the silence. *"I'm sure everything is going to be fine. Johan and Jenna are both strong and determined."* I realize these are just the usual comments one makes to support a friend in need of hope, but I appreciate them anyway. I nod to her, silently chanting a mantra as we speed down the freeway: *"I will get there on time; I will get there on time."* Do I mean in time for the flight, or in time to see Johan before the unthinkable?

Both seem plausible.

I am roused out of my Zen-like chant as we decelerate toward the off-ramp. Soon we will be at the airport with twenty minutes to spare.

I have a sudden surge of energy and clarity, bolstered by my assurance that I will get to the airport on time. I will make my flight. Therefore, I will see Johan. He will survive. Besides, he is too obstinate to die. I know him. I can picture him telling the bear, *"You think you got me? I don't think so."*

This small relief is short-lived.

As we approach a set of railroad tracks between the freeway and the airport, flashing red lights and ringing warning bells announce a train—a really slow train.

I become tearful.

I can't believe this ten-mile-per-hour train, clanking against each rail tie like a ghost dragging a chain, is going to destroy my chances of making it to the airport on time.

Each second drags by like a minute.

We all sit tense, silent, still.

Once again, Laura breaks the silence. *"We still have plenty of time."*

I wonder how many cars are on this damn train, anyway.

The next car is adorned with graffiti art depicting a life-size image of the grim reaper. So immense and detailed is the image that every trace of his dark, shadowed cloak and gleaming scythe is perfectly outlined against the car's steel surface. If I were an author, I could not have dreamt up a more fitting foreshadow.

My eyes—and Laura's—grow huge.

"It doesn't mean anything," Laura bursts out.

Maybe not, but a sense of urgency has returned to my internal chant. *"I will get there on time!"*

The reaper turns out to be one of the last cars on the freight train from hell. Soon we are allowed to finish the remaining four minutes of the drive. I exit the van. I kiss Stephanie and rush to the Frontier Airlines counter.

"I will get there on time!"

My mind is in a haze, yet my body is in overdrive. I give the agent my boarding pass.

"Excuse me, ma'am," a TSA officer motions to me as I stand in line for security check, *"I need to search your bag, ma'am. Please step over to the side."*

What the hell is this? I never get called out for random baggage checks. Full panic mode.

"Ma'am," I say, *"you don't understand, right now my husband is on a life-flight to a trauma center in Seattle. He and my daughter were attackedbyagrizzlybear! I can't miss my flight. This is an extreme emergency—please, must I do this?"*

I am near hysteria.

"I am sorry, ma'am. It is a random check, but it's moving fast."

"Oh my god."

This is not happening.

I am certain to miss my flight.

I heard the boarding call already.

I go through the pat-down.

My bag is handled and brought back to me.

The security guard has some mercy after all.

She has retained a cart and driver to whisk me over to my gate.

"God bless you and good luck, ma'am," says the security officer as she waves me off.

I hop off the cart at my gate.

I am the last one to be seated, but no matter.

I have made it.

I got there on time.

— CHAPTER 1 —
August 25, 2005: Glacier National Park

"A flash of fur, two jumps and 400 pounds of lightning." These words, from a *Los Angeles Times* article masterfully written by Thomas Curwen, vividly encapsulate the first seconds of my experience of being in the wrong place at the wrong time in Glacier National Park on August 25, 2005.

Holy crap, this is weird.

Look at that mean old badger.

Jenna, stay behind me!

What do I do now?

These were the thoughts racing through my mind in the first few moments. The grizzly bear attack would last anywhere between five to fifteen minutes. But time, measured in minutes, made no sense during the attack; it felt at times as though it would never end.

Talk about being in the worst place possible for something like this to happen. Here we were, on an upward sloping leg of Grinnell Glacier Trail, rock cliffs on the right, a vertical drop on the left, and a grizzly bear in my left thigh.

How did we get here?

The perfect confluence of unlikely events, big and small, had conspired to bring us to this place.

We were here because I had wanted to see a grizzly bear—something I had never seen growing up in Holland.

Yes, we made many family trips to Scandinavia, but the biggest animal we had seen even a glimpse of was a moose. Holland (or the Netherlands, technically) is the most densely populated country in Europe. There wasn't much nature left.

Growing up with a brother only about a year younger than me, we had always played together in whatever nature we could find. I am sure I would have decided to become a national park ranger if there had been enough wild places back home, but there weren't. Instead, I became a physical therapist (PT), and because there was no work for me in Holland I had immigrated to the United States. There I met the girl of my dreams, got married, started a family, bought my first house, upgraded to a bigger house and had a great career. The American dream, personified.

But that dream did not include a bear in my thigh.

A bear in my camera or binoculars, certainly, but not this up-close or this personal.

This is going to leave a scar or require some surgery! I remember thinking. *Surgery? I've never even been hospitalized before!*

Where had this story gone wrong?

— CHAPTER 2 —

The Netherlands and the Stubbornness of the Dutch

I grew up in the Netherlands, also known as Holland, in the city of Amsterdam during a particularly colorful time. It was the height of the hippie movement and "flower children" were everywhere, but I was too young to realize what all of this meant. My parents did not really pay attention to that culture either, maybe because they were quite a bit older when they married.

My dad was fifty-four years of age when he married my mother, and she was thirty-nine. I arrived within one year and my brother came fifteen months later. *"We didn't have much time to wait,"* my mom would tell me later, revealing why we arrived so soon after their marriage. Both my brother and I were born into a middle-class family, but that was soon to change.

In my earliest memory, I'm sitting on my dad's lap, and he is throwing a cup of coffee onto the wall above a fireplace. At the same time a man I do not know is running out of our house and then jumping over the backyard fence. Later that day, Dad told me in the front yard of our house in a suburb of Amsterdam that we would have to move because we had lost everything. I did not know what he meant; I was only two or three years of age. But I knew it was something serious, and that my mom was very sad.

Later in life, I discovered the details: My dad had used his life savings to start a car dealership and repair garage in Amsterdam. In so doing, he had signed a business contract with a couple of charlatans who had a huge tax debt. As a result, he went from being financially well off to dirt poor. My parents had no choice but to sell their house and most of their business and move into a rental home in Amsterdam.

My mother hated the big city and vowed to move out as soon as possible. For that reason, our home when I was a child was always quite stark, spare, and sparsely furnished: Why make it comfortable if you are going to move soon anyway?

That "temporary living situation" in the rental turned into an eleven-year stint, and my earliest childhood was spent roaming the streets in the outskirts of Amsterdam, fishing in the canals with my brother, getting into all kinds of big-city sewer dirt filled with God-knows-what-kind-of germs, and building huge bonfires on the streets after Christmas when we would gather the trees into one big stack.

Boys will be boys, as they say, but my mother hated the city's bad influence on us, so every weekend we would drive to the area known as the Polder. The Polder consists of two new pieces of reclaimed land—land that has been created by pumping ocean water out of one area and moving it to another. The Polder held some promise for us since cities and affordable housing were being built there.

So, in the early sixties in a postwar Netherlands, I grew up loving nature. But Holland was developing fast, and as a result, a lot of nature was being lost. As one of the most developed and densely populated countries in the world, there were already no naturally grown forests left. The forests that we did have had been planted by humans. Trees growing in perfect lines seemed artificial and strangely uniform to me. The wildlife seemed monotone as well, and as a child I had already been attracted to wilder places outside the Dutch borders.

My mother knew she had to get her boys out of the city if they were to succeed in life, so she held hope that we might be able to move to the Polder full-time. In the meantime, high school (which in Holland starts when kids are about twelve years old) was a huge struggle for me. I was constantly picked on and bullied by other kids in my class; as the youngest in age by one to two years, I am sure I was immature in my actions. As a sophomore, I barely achieved the grades necessary to pass on to my junior year, and my first report card that junior year was terrible—I had failed at least half of my classes.

Our family finances continued to be horrible as well, until my dad was able to get a stable business going, selling flowers. Very slowly, we crawled out of our dire financial situation, but I still vividly remember my mother turning the pennies around to make sure they were not dimes.

Eventually, my parents were able to get us out of Amsterdam and into a townhouse out on the Polder, in a town called Dronten.

Once we moved to Dronten, everything went much better. Academically, I went from last in my class to first, in one year. That progress opened up more educational opportunities for me, and my mom thought I might be interested in physical therapy as an occupation. (She had been a dental assistant and had a fondness for the medical field.) Now, I knew nothing about physical therapy, and when I mentioned this potential pathway to the student counselor at my school, he was convinced it was too difficult a field for me.

That's all it took for me to want to become a physical therapist.

No one was going to tell me ever again that I couldn't achieve something, which is what the people at my old school had done. (To this day, I am just as steadfast—some might say *stubborn*. If you tell me I can't do something, I will take you up on that challenge and I will achieve it! Of course, when people say I am hard-headed, it reminds me of an old joke about the notorious *stubborn*ness of the Dutch: "Why do Dutch people wear wooden shoes? To keep woodpeckers off their hard wooden heads!" OK, maybe it loses a bit in the translation, but this totally applies to me.)

In truth, Physical Therapy (PT) school was very hard. I was seventeen years of age when I started, and I had to move to Amsterdam to attend the school. Living in Amsterdam—the bad influence—was nearly too much fun to handle for a seventeen-year-old kid, and I barely made it through the first year. In fact, I had to retake six exams in order to pass. That was a huge lesson for me. From that time on I vowed to never let distractions get in the way of achieving my goals.

Stubborn.

For the rest of my schooling, I did very well.

— CHAPTER 3 —
An Immigrant's Story

Contrary to some people's belief, not all immigrants to the United States come from poor countries. I actually do not know any of the immigrants that I hear some politicians talk about, who allegedly come to America to take advantage of the social welfare system. There are a lot of us immigrants, and we come from all over the world, including very rich countries with incredible social welfare systems—countries like the Netherlands.

One thing all immigrants I have ever met have in common is that we all come here to work and to contribute to society.

In Southern California, as I've found out, there are tens of thousands of Dutch immigrants, who attend Dutch reformed churches and own Dutch bakeries. In Orange County, there is even a Dutch club just up the street from the Disneyland resorts.

I did not know any of this when I decided to move to the United States.

In 1983 at age twenty-one I graduated as youngest in my physical therapy (PT) class. But at that time in the Netherlands, there was no work to be found in the field. I must have mailed over three hundred resumes to all kinds of physical therapy businesses, but nothing materialized—except a very part-time job as a trainer for one of the professional basketball teams, Black Velvet. Indeed, the team was named after a brand of Canadian whisky and true to its name, my time with them was incredibly enjoyable.

In addition to attending all their training sessions, helping with taping, stretching, massaging, and whatever else was necessary for the success of the team, I became the team's number one fan. My enthusiasm for the guys was such that I even earned a technical foul once for being far too loud as I protested a referee call. I was just barely paid for my services—twenty-five guilders (approximately ten US dollars) in cash per game, as I remember—but that was not the point. The point was that I was getting some experience as a physical therapist.

Although I enjoyed being a team trainer, I still wanted a "real job." A friend of mine in California mentioned that the hiring situation for physical therapists in the United States was completely different from the Netherlands. On a whim, just to find out what the possibilities might be, I applied to some jobs that were posted in the American Physical Therapy Association's magazine. To my surprise, responses were favorable. Some businesses stated they would even give assistance with obtaining a green card (permanent resident card and work permit) and attorney fees if I were eventually hired.

Since I had received no positive responses on any letters and applications I had sent out to PT practices in Holland, I decided to give immigrating to the United States a serious try. In order to do that, I contacted an agency that actively recruited Dutch physical therapists to work in the United States. I met with one of their agents and we had a great interview. But there was a catch: the only places they were looking to hire people were Ohio and Illinois.

I had no intention of leaving the wet and miserable weather in Holland to replace it with similarly miserable weather on another continent. If I was going to go through the expense and legal hurdles of immigrating, I wanted to land where there was warm weather instead. So I mentioned to the recruiter that I wanted to move to California.

"That is not possible."

Well. You simply don't tell me something is not possible. I knew for a fact it must be possible. So, I said goodbye and took my job hunting and immigration efforts into my own hands.

I contacted the California State Board to find out what a foreign-trained therapist had to do to get a license. Then I went on a translation binge with a great friend of mine. We translated everything related to my schooling in the Netherlands into English. I went back all the way to elementary school and got representatives from grade school, high school, and PT school to sign authentication documents verifying that what I had translated was true and correct. I sent the resulting (enormous) package to the consumer affairs department in California and applied to sit for the state board exam in California. To my surprise, they had no further questions, and in July of 1984, I was accepted to take the test.

I was on my way!

But now there were a few details to be taken care of, such as, *"Where do I stay in California?"* and *"Mom and Dad, can I borrow some money?"* and, of course, *"How do I get a visa?"*

The first detail was easy: I was lucky. I had a friend from the Netherlands who was already living in Los Angeles, and she and her boyfriend said they would be happy to have me stay with them while I determined whether a move to the United States was possible, and what I really wanted.

One down.

Next up: My mom and dad did not want to see me leave home, but they understood, and would lend me about $2,000. That was close to 6,000 guilders at that time—a lot of money for my parents.

Two down.

Now for the more difficult part: I needed a visa to get to California to take the test.

I had heard that the American consulate was pretty picky about tourist visas. That was true, and in my case, they assumed (more or less correctly) that because I was unemployed, my intentions were to move to the United States. I guess I was that obvious. And so, the consulate rejected my initial request for a visa.

But…*stubborn.*

I protested. I had to get a letter from my current employer (the basketball club) and my mother stating that I had obligations in Holland and had to come back. In addition, I had to buy a return airplane ticket. My friend also advised me to try to go through US customs in a place other than Los Angeles, so I would not get stopped at the airport. My first flight to the United States came in to Minneapolis. I went through customs at that airport, where I had to state the reason for my visit—which was, of course, "vacation." Certainly it was not "sitting for the California State Physical Therapy Board exam in Los Angeles a few days from now."

I arrived in Los Angeles with a suitcase and $1,000 in hand. The other $1,000 I'd had to spend on an airline ticket. My friend and her boyfriend picked me up at the airport and they drove me to their home.

I was in awe of Los Angeles. The freeways were huge and wide open. Finally, I was in a city with no traffic—in Amsterdam it was always gridlocked! (I had arrived when the 1984 Olympic games were about to kick off, and to everyone's surprise, the city had emptied out. We had a few weeks of no-traffic bliss until the worse-than-Amsterdam gridlock reappeared.)

We drove past downtown. It was astounding and so incredibly big. I had never seen anything like it close-up. After the initial wave of wonder and amazement, jet lag was getting to me—I had to crash. Right around the time I was falling asleep, the phone rang at my friend's house. A woman who owned a PT practice was wondering if I was looking for a job. (Actually, I was looking for a good night's sleep, but my friend had turned out to be right—this was the Promised Land! There were jobs for me everywhere!) I told the lady I would get back to her after my State Board Exam a few days later.

Those State Boards were not as easy as I thought they would be.

The exam was held in the Ambassador Hotel in Los Angeles—the same place Robert Kennedy had been shot.

I decided to walk there from the place my friends lived in West Hollywood. The true meaning of the saying "Nobody walks in LA" became clear to me very quickly. I was the only person walking up Wilshire Boulevard that morning. People in cars would look at me with a "what is he doing?" expression, when I could actually see their faces. After a few times of crossing the street I learned pedestrians must watch out for motorists that pay no attention to them. Very different from Amsterdam.

The test itself was a morning and an afternoon event. I started talking with two young women also there to take the test, one from Oregon and one from New Zealand. I had lunch with them and we were all commiserating about the morning exam. Having to take the test in English was kind of difficult for me. There had been at least twenty questions where I did not understand what the test was asking, so I'd had to guess.

At lunch, one of my new "study buddies" asked me what my sign was. "I don't know what that means—I am Dutch."

"No," she said, "Your birth sign…"

"Oh, OK, well, I am a Virgin."

They both busted out laughing. The young lady from New Zealand asked, "Can we help you with that?" I imagine I must have turned every shade of red a face could turn as they laughed, and then they explained the correct term was "Virgo."

The afternoon test was just as difficult as the morning session and I swore the best answer to the first ten or so questions was "C." Of course, that couldn't be, because normally test makers do not design exams with the same correct answer to so many questions in a row. While I was thinking that and staring in front of me someone lifted his answer sheet to put it next to him, and I could see that he had answered a lot of questions all in the same row as well. I could not see whether it was A, B, C, or D, but it was definitely a block of the same answers! From then on, I simply trusted my gut to choose answers.

I walked out thinking I had not passed the exam, and when I came home I told my friends that I'd better start studying for the next one. In the meantime, the woman who had called me the evening of my arrival kept pursuing me; when I told her I may not have passed the exam she did not seem to care. She would have a job for me regardless. I had no clue that you could not work with a tourist visa and no Social Security card, but this simply goes to show you that it was very easy for undocumented people to get work.

Something told me this wasn't all above-board. I did not pursue anything with this person, but instead contacted local hospitals. I was interviewed at several and it wasn't until I went to San Gabriel

Medical Center that the rehab manager told me that to be eligible to work legally in the United States I must pass the test and that the hospital would need to be willing to sponsor me for a work permit.

I was so lucky. Only a few weeks later, I learned that I had passed the test and in September, 1984, I started working at San Gabriel Valley Medical Center, where I met my future wife, Marilyn.

— CHAPTER 4 —
A Family's Story

My time at San Gabriel Valley Medical Center (SGVMC) was extremely valuable to my career development. I gained expertise in treating people in a variety of settings including acute care, rehabilitation, outpatient care, and home health. Being a physical therapist is an amazing job and you become quite the expert in anatomy and movement. You know all the muscles, joints and bones with their individual muscle and tendon attachments, and you become very good in palpation, or "feeling" skills. You have to touch people continuously, so after a few years of practicing it's quite natural to be adept at determining when something is not moving correctly.

Meanwhile, I had fallen head over heels in love with Marilyn, and soon we were engaged.

I first saw Marilyn during my interview at SGVMC. She came in to the Human Resources office to ask for some time off because her sister was getting married, and I was immediately struck by how beautiful she was. She already had a boyfriend, I later learned from my new coworkers, but that didn't stop me from becoming great friends with her. We had the same sense of humor and sensibilities, and soon we were spending lunches or other work-related activities together like any other work buddies would.

Luckily for me, she and her boyfriend broke up after about a year and a half. I didn't wait very long before I told her that I cared more about her than just being a work friend. It turned out she felt the same, and for the next year and a half while we dated, I knew she was the one. Marilyn needed some convincing; but again, I'm *stubborn*, and she grew fonder of me as well.

Marilyn's parents, on the other hand, loved me from the moment they saw me. Steve (her dad) was from Croatia, so another European was great! He started to treat me like his son-in-law pretty much immediately. Violet (her mother) was a lovely sweet lady; somehow we connected immediately as well.

We got married in the Croatian church in downtown Los Angeles, just as Steve wanted it. Since he was paying the bill, it kind of became his party. I just went with the flow.

My parents came from the Netherlands for the wedding, along with my brother and his girlfriend. This was the first time they would meet Marilyn. It was also the first time flying for my parents. My eighty-year-old dad loved it. Yes, they were quite nervous at first, but the minute they settled down and were served, their fears disappeared.

I wasn't nervous at all about them meeting Marilyn because I knew they would like her. But what made them really like Marilyn right away were her parents. It was very important to my parents that she came from a normal family just like they were. Although they did not speak each other's languages, they got along right away. My dad was quite the character and could let his feelings be known in any language by gesturing and acting out what he wanted.

Unfortunately, this was to be the first and last time that Marilyn got to see my dad. Seven months after the wedding, he passed away suddenly from cardiac failure. I was devastated. I'd wanted him to meet his first grandchild.

He did get to see the first picture of baby Jenna smiling, however, and he loved that smiley little baby. We buried him with that picture of Jenna on his chest.

My mother was devastated by his death, and Marilyn and I convinced her to come spend the following winter with us. That way she would be in a sunny location and away from her memories. My mother ended up making that a routine. For the next eight years, she would spend every winter with us cooking, cleaning, and taking care of the kids, if necessary. Unfortunately, that came to an end when she was diagnosed with multiple myeloma while here in the United States one winter, and passed away seven months later at home in Holland.

Steve and Violet became my parents, but that also came to an end when Steve was diagnosed with end-stage colon cancer, which took his life when he was only in his seventies. (Violet was still around when Jenna and I were attacked by the grizzly, though she was in her eighties and frail. She chuckled when she saw me with a bald head for the first time, and said she thought that was kind of sexy! What a sweet thing to say, and also, how hip, because…well, of course she was correct. Bald heads had by now become the in thing, and she made me feel great with that one little comment.)

After Marilyn and I married, and with a new baby on the way, we wanted to buy our own house, but Los Angeles properties were not affordable. We moved into the little extra house in the back of my in-laws' house for two years so we could save our rent money and be able to buy our own house. We ultimately settled about twenty-five miles northeast of San Diego, in a town called Escondido.

Marilyn hated it.

As a city girl, she wanted to be close to culture and entertainment. Escondido had none of that, in her view. I loved it. As a child who had only bad memories of growing up in a city, I wanted my family to grow up in a more rural setting. I wanted to garden, raise animals and have a house where we did not have to hear the neighbors through the walls. Ultimately, Escondido was what we could afford. That was the deal, and we settled on an older house with character and a third of an acre of land.

After a few years Marilyn had gotten more used to living "in the country." With the inheritance from my mother, we were able to move to a great school district and the home where we still live today.

The girls rounded out the family.

I still remember seeing Jenna as a newborn, cleaned up in the hospital nursery, seemingly asleep on her left side. She was only one day old, yet very aware of her surroundings—when another baby cried, Jenna just opened her right eye and gave a look that seemed to say, *"Oh please, can you be quiet? I'm trying to sleep here."* Jenna already seemed wise beyond the twenty-four hours that she had been outside her mother's womb. Jenna was the perfect baby, although she refused to sleep. As an infant, I had to carry her around until she finally dozed off, or take her for a car ride. Otherwise, she behaved perfectly. She never fussed around when taken to a restaurant or other public area. People used to come up to us and tell us what a perfect baby we had.

Stephanie came two-and-a-half years later and was more the typical baby, loud in public places and occasionally throwing a temper tantrum, especially during the "terrible twos." Neither girl was difficult, though. And Stephanie was actually very easy to get to sleep. When she was tired she would sleep, no fussing. Jenna would fight sleep to the point that she once fell face-forward into her dinner, asleep, still mumbling that she was not tired.

Marilyn had an aunt, Aunt Marilyn (whom she was obviously named after) who had been a professional dancer. Jenna was enthralled by her and we thought that dance would probably be a great routine for her as well. When she was barely five, I took her to a local dance studio, where I had her observe a dance class. She was entranced. For the next twenty years, until she went to medical school, dance became a very important part of her life.

Of course younger sister Stephanie wanted to do what her older sister was doing, and soon we had both girls in dance, going to competitions and performances on many a Saturday.

In high school, Jenna tried out for the dance team and was thrilled to make it onto the varsity team right away. Stephanie followed in her older sister's footsteps, which made it super easy for Marilyn and me, because the extra-curricular activities were usually the same for both girls. The dance team and the parents of the dance team became an important part of our lives for more than six years.

We were a busy and boring normal family. At least we were in the days when our kids were still in high school. A typical Saturday would start like this: Marilyn and Johan would be up by 6:30 a.m., which actually constitutes "sleeping in" for both. The whir of the coffee bean grinder, the clink of the glass coffee pot as its edges hit the sink, and the crash of dishes being taken out of the dishwasher and replaced in cupboards could be heard a few minutes later. Inevitably, one of the girls, usually Steph, would grumpily come downstairs asking, *"Can't you guys be a little more quiet? It's so early."* Then she'd flop on the couch in the family room and turn on the TV while our little dog Noel snuggled next to her. Cici, the cat, would purr somewhere nearby.

We did not usually eat breakfast all together on Saturdays because I wanted to get to my yard chores. Marilyn ate whenever she got up, and the girls both had their own wakeup schedules. Marilyn usually took the time to fix a hot breakfast for Steph, because she liked the pampering. I actually enjoyed it too. But Jenna wanted to be left to her own wiles for breakfast and usually she'd pick all the "healthy" foods, leaving none for the rest of us. Honest. Then she'd usually be off to a dance class of some sort at the local studio in town. Steph would join her later.

In the meantime, Marilyn and I would walk the dog and then get on with our weekend rituals of yardwork and housecleaning.

Our house sits on 1.3 useable acres. It was a blank canvas when we moved there—just weeds and a couple of citrus trees. Fast-forward a few years, though, and every square foot was cultivated, drip irrigated, and planted.

My rule in the yard is that everything, once established, needs to be as drought-tolerant as possible, and I need to be able to eat an edible fruit from my own yard any time of the year. With farm blood running through my veins from both my parents' sides, I also like to grow so much that I can share the bounty at work. I am known to arrive in the morning with crates of peaches, plums, oranges, or grapefruits.

In addition, I used my yard to expand my birdwatching (and raising) hobby quite a bit. I built enough birdhouses to breed everything that does not make too much noise, can't kill you, and thrives in a captive environment. We have chickens, little finches in huge aviaries, and a variety of parrots that have been captive-bred for many years. I belong to nearly all the bird clubs in the county, and enjoy mingling with people from all walks of life. Often we have just one thing in common—our love of birds.

The Road to Glacier National Park

While the kids were growing up, we went on little trips that became bigger trips all the time. Even when Jenna was a baby, we took her up the California coast to the Redwood National and State Parks. There is not one park in the Southwestern United States that we have not visited at least once.

Jenna was only four years old and Stephanie one year when we took them on our first big road trip to Yellowstone National Park. What a trip that was. Only two hours on our way, going up Interstate 15 at the Cajon Pass (a notoriously steep section of road), the car started to overheat. I thought it was a fluke. Not so.

Right outside of Baker (the necessary gas stop on the way to Las Vegas) we became one of those families standing alongside the highway with steam coming out from under the hood. We were able to carry on, driving fifty miles an hour and coasting as fast as we could on downhill stretches all the way to just outside of Cedar City, Utah.

I was determined to make Salt Lake City on our first day. Because *stubborn*.

The radiator had other plans.

Luckily, we found a garage that on the Saturday night of Labor Day weekend was willing and able to temporarily fix our radiator and thermostat. We made Salt Lake City at 11:30 p.m. The little girls jumped for joy on the hotel beds.

The next day the intent was to make it into Yellowstone and yet again, we had to cool the car down a few times before we finally made it. Driving around Yellowstone and Grand Teton National Parks turned out to be fine, but on the way back home, we drove fifty miles an hour on most stretches, with the heater on to get rid of some of the engine heat, all windows open, in 110-degree heat. We had to stop and cool down the car many times, but we made it!

Never again would we take a trip like that with an old car. But we made many trips like this over the ensuing years. I think that way we truly instilled a love for the great outdoors and adventure in both of our girls, along with an appreciation for the beauty of the western United States. Marilyn and I also took the girls on individual road trips if the other couldn't come for some reason. Jenna especially enjoyed the trips we made to Holland to visit friends and family.

Jenna and I had planned a graduation trip to the Grand Teton and Glacier National Parks after she graduated high school. She had done very well and was one of the kids that graduated the highest in her class—valedictorian circle status.

August seemed like a great month to make this graduation trip, just the two of us. In previous years when Jenna and I had traveled together to the Netherlands, we were good traveling companions. We both always wanted to see what was behind the mountain, beyond the next curve, and we both were quite physically fit.

Being more of an introvert, Jenna likes hiking because it gives her a chance to clear her head, relieve stress, and just enjoy the raw beauty of nature. I have those same feelings, yet being an extrovert, I like to voice those thoughts through words and photographs. When I hike, I take pictures of everything—maybe in the back of my mind, I think I can create the next Ansel Adams-like masterpiece. And of course through photos, I can also share every moment of our trip with anyone who wants to see it later, while I relive my adventures over and over again.

That first day of our trip, Jenna and I left in the late afternoon to get a head start before traffic set in; plus, we also hoped to make it through the California and Nevada desert during the least hot part of the day. We planned to get all the way to Cedar City, Utah, and arrive in Jackson Hole, Wyoming the next day. We certainly made that goal, although we did get pulled over a few hundred yards before our exit from the freeway (allegedly, we'd been speeding in a construction zone; neither Jenna nor I had seen any signs posted, but the truck we'd been driving behind probably blocked our view). The officer was very nice and could see from our faces that we hadn't been speeding on purpose. Nevertheless, he slapped us with an eighty-five dollar fine and sent us on our way.

The next morning, we drove all the way to Jackson Hole. Since we were able to check into our motel early, we had time to drive into Grand Teton National Park for a few minutes and observe our first elk and antelope. Several hikes and days later, we felt well prepared to tackle Glacier National Park, so up and over we drove.

As we got closer and closer to the park from the east side, we saw more and more clouds. Weather is quite unpredictable in the northern Rockies any time of year, and we saw that we would not have the best weather on the day of our arrival. By the time we checked into the Swift Current Lodge in the Many Glaciers area, the weather was cold and rainy.

We spent the obligatory amount of minutes and dollars buying souvenirs in the hotel gift shop; I just had to buy one of the *Bear Attacks of the Century* books that contained short stories about grizzly and black bear attacks. Must be the little boy in me, but I've always liked to read that kind of stuff.

After a great night's sleep, we awoke the following morning to inclement weather. Again.

Since we could not really hike, Jenna and I decided to spend that day driving to the various park sites, such as the Going to the Sun Road and Goat Lick. As we drove, the weather went from rain to snow. How exciting was that, since this was August, and who would expect snow in the summer? Of course I had to stop at Logan Pass and get my picture taken in the snow.

That became quite a famous shot; it was the last time I was photographed with hair.

August 24 on Logan Pass—the last picture I have with hair.

CHAPTER 4

In Apgar Village, at the foot of Lake McDonald, we stopped again to wander around, and from there we drove around the park via Goat Lick—which should simply be called "Lick," since one hardly ever sees goats there. I grew more excited at the possibility of seeing big wild animals all around us.

Driving back to the east side of the divide, I realized how fascinating it was to see the differences in Glacier National Park on each side of the continental divide.

The continental divide is so named because it divides which direction rainwater flows. It flows to the Atlantic Ocean if it falls on the east side, and the Pacific Ocean if it falls on the west side, or to the Hudson Bay area if it falls on the north side. Indeed, there aren't just two sides to this divide: because some portions have a north side, there it's called the triple divide.

From a tourist perspective, it doesn't really matter where the water flows, but you see major landscape differences. The west side of the divide is where the mountainsides face the storms that come in with the jet stream from the Pacific Ocean and is therefore wetter, more lush and a bit warmer. Trees grow much bigger on the west side, and, as a result, it is harder to spot any wildlife. The west side is also more developed, with some towns, such as Kalispell, that resemble "Anytown, USA," with all the conveniences and chain retail stores available.

When you cross the divide, the landscape is more wild. You can see more rock formations. The landscape opens up, and so it is easier to see moose, bear, goats, sheep, and deer. The human population is sparser, with the biggest town being Browning. That's where the prairies start. This is the Blackfoot Indian Nation country. I often joke that you can see Chicago from there, because it is so flat and there are no trees to speak of. It has its own beauty, and I prefer this side of the park because of its wilder nature.

Temperatures are more extreme on the east side of the park, since in the winter either the hot winds known as the Chinook come down from Canada or arctic blasts come down from the north. That creates a harsh environment, and as a result the vegetation does not grow as tall in most spots. The east side of the divide is the least like the Netherlands, and therefore I am attracted to it the most.

That evening, we devised a plan for the following day. If the weather turned out to be good for hiking, we would hike up to the Grinnell Glacier in the morning and over to Iceberg Lake in the afternoon. We would hike up to the Grinnell Glacier in the morning and over to Iceberg Lake in the afternoon. I wanted to start at daybreak, but Jenna reminded me that this was bear country, and that we should hike during "office hours." By that she meant office hours for normal people, since my office hours always start at daybreak, after a run.

▶ A Side Note on Running

It is 2:15 a.m. (or earlier) and I wake up. Within forty-five minutes, I will have checked my e-mails, had a cup of coffee, and checked the morning news from Holland, since they are nine hours ahead of the United States.

Now I am ready to hit the streets of San Diego for my weekday morning run. My runs are not what you'd call jogs.

I run at least five miles every weekday morning, and once a week, one of those runs covers anywhere from twelve to twenty-two miles, depending on where I am with my training schedule for the next marathon. Once I get back home I may do some weight training. Then I shower and change into my work clothes. By 6 a.m. I hope to be at my desk at work in La Jolla—a twenty-five-minute drive from my home at that hour, but a forty-five to fifty-five-minute drive any later than that.

I have been faithful to this routine since I started working at Scripps Health in 1992 as the Director for Sports Medicine. Running was never something I did for fun while growing up. Back then, exercise meant work. Growing up in the Netherlands, we exercised because we had to. My high school was about ten miles away from home, and during the warmer months we biked to school. That was enough exercise. During the summer or fall vacation, I worked for the local farmers doing anything from weeding acres of potatoes, sugar beets and the like, or picking apples. That was plenty of physical activity for anyone, I figured.

But being in charge of a sports medicine department and not doing any sports myself seemed somehow wrong to me. That is how I decided to start running. It was something I could do by myself without too much equipment, and no one would have to watch me do it and see how terrible I was. And it turned out that I wasn't terrible at all.

The first run I ever did lasted about twenty minutes and felt easy. Slowly I worked up to doing thirty minutes, and then sixty minutes. Once the word was out that I enjoyed running, some of the people I worked with told me that I should come run a half-marathon with them. That gave me a goal.

Stubborn.

For the next few months I was able to work up to running for about ninety minutes. That first half-marathon, the America's Finest City run in San Diego, was very exciting.

In the shuttle bus on the way over to the starting line was an "older" gentleman in his early sixties who was using the event as a training run for a whole marathon. I thought he was crazy.

Ninety or so minutes later, I crossed my very first half-marathon finish line and saw Marilyn and my daughters waiting for me. As I dragged myself over the finish line and walked over to my family, I couldn't imagine turning around and doing that whole distance one more time. But I guess Marilyn knew me better than I knew myself; she told me she suspected I would be running full marathons soon. *"No way!"* I thought, yet a few years later the first Rock 'n' Roll marathon was planned in San Diego and I challenged myself to try it.

Stubborn.

When I finished that first marathon, I was elated.

Although I'd experienced pain and exhaustion during the final two miles, I felt sheer joy in knowing that I could actually accomplish this. I was hooked. I have run every Rock 'n' Roll San Diego Marathon along with more than fifty other marathons, eight of them in Boston.

Running is important to me, both for my mental and physical health. My early morning runs help me to relax. I sometimes get so lost in my thoughts I literally forget where I've run. You might think that I'd get tired of awakening at 2:30 a.m. every weekday morning just so I can run. But my early morning mantra of *"Come on, you're not seventy yet,"* seems to motivate me to get vertical, shuffle downstairs, and get going.

Stubborn.

At 2:30 in the morning, I do not often see other runners, but I do see many animals. My most exciting spotting was when I nearly ran into a bobcat on the campus of the University of California, San Diego, which is right across the freeway from the hospital where I worked for many years and linked by an overpass. (What is it with me and running into animals?)

I have also become well acquainted with individual beat police officers, paper delivery guys, and the security patrol in certain areas, who often wave at me. Running in the dark reveals a whole new world, and it is beautiful. I have seen far away lightning storms, the orange glow of wildfires in distant mountains, and the full moon reflecting off the ocean.

Running in the morning in new cities is also exciting, and I often check out places that I may want to return to later on during daylight. The first time I ran in Washington, DC I decided to go to the National Mall and check out all the monuments. Little did I know that I could actually just walk up to these famous places so early in the morning. I was completely awestruck when I saw the Lincoln Memorial in the early morning hours. And it was a surreal experience to see the marching soldiers depicted in the Korean War Memorial against the early morning fog over the Potomac River.

I will continue to run marathons for as long as I can. Pushing your body to run for this distance makes everything seem easier; nothing is as hard physically than the last six miles of a marathon when you want to run a specific time. By now I can easily run the 26.2 miles, and I have even done a few thirty-plus milers. But to achieve a particular time goal, that's difficult, because you need to keep pace regardless of how much you want to walk—or quit.

Of course, during an official marathon race, I love the exuberance of the spectators, the musical acts and the landscape. It helps me keep a steady rhythm and it takes the monotony out of running 26.2 miles. Often I am amazed by the other participants and always wonder how someone in an Elvis costume wearing a polyester leisure suit and wig can possibly be faster than me. On the other hand, I also pass many people only half my age.

In Glacier National Park, on the day of the attack, it turns out running did something else for me.

Long after that day, Gary, the park ranger who kept me calm and sat by my side in the immediate hours after the bear ripped into my head, arm, and leg told me, "If you had not been a marathon runner, I am not sure you would have survived."

Gary told me that while he was keeping me stable on the mountain, my blood pressure dropped dangerously low—so low he could barely detect it anymore. This was most likely due to losing so much blood. I was awake and joking at the time, so he had to assume I was doing OK, but in reality I was slowly slipping away.

Luckily, the years of marathon running had trained my body to respond to this severe situation just like it would respond to the extreme demands of the last six miles of a marathon. When you think your body really can't do it any longer, somehow your mind takes over and convinces you to make it.

Along the Boston Marathon route, there's a sign that reads, "OK, legs. Time for the brain to take over."

On that mountain, on that day, both my brain and my body were able to keep me going beyond what should have been possible. Marathon running may have saved my life.

The Early/Late Start to Grinnell Trail

Between my "office hours" and the rest of the world's "office hours," Jenna and I compromised; we'd start at 7:30 a.m. rather than 8:00.

Convincing Jenna to start early was a bit difficult, though, because the night before, when we had walked to dinner at the Swift Current Lodge, we had passed within a few dozen feet of a fairly large black bear. He had completely ignored us (and many other walkers). Instead, he was occupied with eating huckleberries or something else growing low to the ground in the Many Glacier area.

While August 24 had been rainy and snowy, August 25 started out beautiful, chilly and damp. Patches of blue dotted the sky, and the weather predictions were favorable. We packed my backpack with plenty of water, some trail mix, a can of bear spray that I had bought in San Diego, and my video and camera gear.

Whenever I hiked, I always took a small video recorder and my camera—much to the annoyance of my family. (I still do to this day, only now it's also my iPhone). As a result, hiking for me becomes interval training because I continuously stop to admire some object, big or small, and take pictures of it. Then I have to run and catch up with my fellow hikers.

This day was no different.

As usual, Jenna was getting a bit annoyed with me and several times told me to hurry up or we would not be able to do the afternoon hike. If there is anything worse for me than not getting a picture of something while hiking, it's not completing the plan for that day, regardless of how outrageously difficult that plan is. So, although I was admiring a golden eagle soaring overhead and wanted to try to film it, I left my camera off and hurried to catch up with Jenna, who was the pacesetter and leader of this hike.

The Grinnell Trail is absolutely gorgeous. The trailhead begins at a parking lot, and when we started out, there was only one other car in the lot. That meant we would be one of the first on the trail! The first to walk though damp, dew-dripping spider webs and on moist pine needles.

Grinnell Trail starts out easy; there is a self-interpretive nature walk at its beginning point. Visitors can donate a quarter and take a flyer that explains the different plants and trees on the trail, which include lodge pole pines and aspen trees.

As soon as we walked into the woods, we were greeted by a man going for a morning stroll with a cup of coffee in his hands. Fortunately, he was the only interruption, and soon I could lapse back to my romantic notion of nature.

Signs at the start of the Grinnell Trail

One thing I realized (probably a bit too late, as the realization came to me after the attack) is the fact that when you get onto a trail in Glacier National Park, you step into wilderness and maybe even back in time. There is no cell phone or other access to a wireless world while walking in a few-million-acre natural zoo where the animals freely roam. In fact, people are the species being observed there as they hike with their wilderness gear on.

Hiking in that environment makes me feel as if I'm in a place where I truly belong. My senses become more acute; I hear sounds that I normally do not pay attention to; I look at everything, big or small, and I pick up on all the different scents of nature. Stepping into a Montana forest early in the morning smells as much like home to me as when other people come home for the holidays while mom is baking Christmas cookies. The scent is like fresh firewood with a hint of pine resin.

It is very easy to romanticize nature that way and lull yourself into a false sense of security, as I certainly did.

Our bear spray was neatly packed into a side pocket of my backpack, not easily accessible unless I could maneuver my arm backwards like a contortionist (I can't).

After all, there would be no way we would need to use that anyway.

Did I mention Jenna did not have any bear spray, or a back pack, so as not to burden her with too heavy a load while she enjoyed the hike?

We also hiked very quietly so as not to scare the wildlife; that way, we reasoned, we could possibly catch an easier view of an animal.

In short, we made almost every mistake possible when hiking in the wilderness.

In order to be truly prepared and the most safe when you are walking among the three-hundred-fifty-plus grizzly bears that call Glacier home (and let's not forget the numerous moose and black bears that are also known to be quite dangerous), it isn't enough to just have proper equipment and random facts about what to do in a potentially dangerous situation. You also have to know how to use that equipment and those facts.

Anyway, at this point in time, ignorance was bliss, and we hiked without a care in the world toward Grinnell Glacier on one of the most popular hikes in the park. I knew that a naturalist-led hiking group would be on the trail around 9:00 a.m., and therefore wanted to make sure we were ahead of them so they would not slow us down or scare away any animals.

What a foolish mistake. Alerting animals to your presence by making noise is exactly what people should be doing when walking in a park with roaming grizzlies. (Not that grizzly bears—or any other animals, for that matter—are out to get you. On the contrary, they're just going about their daily routines of eating, traveling, maybe mating if it is the right time of year. Depending on their size, they may stand their ground, attack, or run away if a hiker disturbs them.)

Being loud warns animals that something is coming toward them that may disturb their routine, and what would any decent animal do in that case except pause, move out of the way, or let their presence be known so no one gets hurt? In normal circumstances, every animal prefers survival and safety, because for either hunter or prey, being hurt means possible death—something we all want to avoid.

But what happens when you startle someone? The fight-or-flight response kicks in and someone may get hurt.

As we continued our hike, we heard the sound of trickling water making its way down the valley toward the beautiful turquoise lakes. The air was calm and the wind was gently blowing around the top of the trees. Down on the forest floor, the air was still. After a few miles of trail that wound through pristine lakeside forests, we found ourselves up on a beautiful hillside with brush and patches of Alpine Fir trees. The brush looks deceivingly short, yet anyone who tries to bushwhack their way through this stuff would soon realize that some of it is over six feet tall, full of branches that can be a tangled mess, with nettles that are not so pleasant to brush against.

From lush brush-covered slopes the trail continued up and up, exposing more and more meadow-like areas and rocky slopes. The turquoise lakes at the bottom of the valley seemed more vivid the further up we went, and the view of Lake Grinnell became absolutely stunning as this day slowly turned into a nice sunny morning.

The last two pictures I took show Jenna with the stunning landscape

As the pacesetter, Jenna kept a few steps ahead of me. She'd decided to take the lead after I'd kind of lost the trail a few times back at Grand Teton National Park. On one particular trail, I had misread the landscape and started to follow an old goat trail that quickly turned into a rock scramble for us until we found the actual trail again. Jenna therefore felt she was more suited to lead. For picture-taking purposes, I also liked to stay in the follower position, so I was able to get as many shots of the landscape as possible. The golden eagle soaring overhead begging to be filmed was just one of many.

▶ A Brief Word about Birds

When it comes to birds, what's not to love?

Birds have been a part of my life as long as I can remember. They provide the perfect point of entry to the natural world.

When I lived in the city, birds were the creatures that kept me connected to nature. No matter how much cold, urban development there was around me, birds reminded me I was still a part of the natural world. In the springtime, I would visit a lake or a park and see mother ducks with their hungry little ducklings, all of them eating anything we threw their way.

A mother duck starting out with ten or more ducklings nearly always ended up with just a handful of grown fledglings. Rats, big fish, cats and herons would take their share of the cute little birds. Nature was teaching me a lesson: some of us survive and move on to live a full life, others are not meant to live a long life.

Birds seem to ground me (no pun intended). They remind me of a world that is bigger than myself, and they keep me humble. Perhaps that is why I also became a keeper and breeder of birds; they teach me lessons.

My birds are a major hobby. I breed everything that does not make too much noise, from African Greys to little finches. I have bred birds since I was thirteen years old and always had a few caged birds, but since I now have a house and large yard, the hobby has expanded exponentially. I must have around three hundred birds now.

My birds are solely dependent on me for their food and shelter, but they reward me with their exuberance. They remind me how much I love life.

The birds I keep, I keep in my aviaries so they retain much more of their wild characteristics. Just like people, some birds are easier to please than others, and I love the challenge of being able to reproduce them successfully. If I can't seem to get them to mate and raise babies, I will try to read as much about their natural environment as possible and will try to reproduce that. If I can't do that, I will not continue to have those birds in my aviaries, because if I cannot make them 100 percent happy, I don't want to keep them caged and unhappy.

Regardless of how easy or difficult my birds are to please, I love sitting among them, watching them as they enjoy the wild grasses that I have collected for them from my yard, where I know no herbicides have been used.

My passion for birds is not restricted to captive breeding; I have also retained my love of birdwatching since childhood. I'm birding whenever I am outside or, failing that, wherever there's a window.

Our yard is planted with fruiting trees and plants that produce during different seasons, so there is always something to eat for us humans, but also for the birds. I participate in an annual ritual called Feeder Watch, operated by Cornell University, in which citizen scientists contribute to a large research base in regard to how many birds and what kinds of birds visit our feeders in the winter. Even outside our yard, I always have to look at birds and see if I recognize a bird that I may not ever have seen before. Like many bird-watchers, we keep a lifetime list of birds and we would like to see as many birds as possible. I am sure the birds watch us as well, and they see even more than we do.

It's remarkable to me to reflect, therefore, that the golden eagle I was filming in Glacier had already seen the grizzly bear on the trail ahead of us.

Back on the Trail

"Hurry up, Dad, or we're not going to make it on time," Jenna called to me. She was right. I had spent way too much time filming the eagle, so I stowed my camera and hiked up the trail to get closer to her.

Earlier during our hike, we had been "oohing" and "aahing" about the splendor of this park. We'd talked about what we would like to do for the rest of our trip.

I had also been strategizing about other things in my head—primarily, thinking of ways I could qualify for the Boston marathon again. I had run it a few times and kind of slacked off from my training and needed another sub-3:30 time to qualify. The Long Beach marathon was coming up; I figured with all this hiking at high elevations, I might be prepared to add some speed work at home.

Walking quickly towards Jenna, I caught up with her and we started the steeper part of our hike. With rocks on the right and a sheer cliff on the left, there seemed no need to be looking for animals because (I reasoned) no animal would be close to us in this narrow, boxed-in spot anyway.

The wind blew into our faces, which felt great. It was slowly getting warmer (in the high 50s) and we were now keeping a pretty fast hiking pace.

Water was dripping off the rocks around us and tiny hanging gardens were everywhere.

Jenna readied herself to go around a curve to the right on the trail.

— CHAPTER 5 —

Life Interrupted

Jenna yelled and stepped back simultaneously.

Then she was running and falling away from something.

Acting instinctively, I threw myself in front of her. Something brown raced toward me. I saw light teeth and claws against a dark brown background. *What kind of a mean old badger is this?*

The "badger" hit me in the face and left thigh.

My daughter was behind me, so I stood my ground.

I thought to myself, *"I am as solid as a rock and strong; nothing is going to come through me with Jenna behind me."*

Exactly what I saw—plus I saw claws.

The "badger" hits me again.

I realize that it isn't hitting me—it's biting me!

I see blood, yet I feel no pain.

I have no fear. I'm standing very solidly.

All this happens in the span of 0.5 seconds.

For the first time in my life I realize what a strange concept time actually is. In the first second of the attack, time crawled. There was a void between 0 and 0.2 seconds.

Then between 0.2 and 0.7 seconds there was this thing coming at me. Impact occurred.

After that, everything seemed to go in slow motion (as you so often hear from others when they go through a traumatic event such as a car crash).

The second bite seemed to happen quickly, but I still felt as if we were stuck in a sea of thick honey or molasses.

It seemed to take forever for me to look down and determine what had bitten me, yet when I saw the brown grizzled coat I knew this was a bear. And not just any bear—a grizzly bear. We had inadvertently caused it to attack because we had gotten too close.

Standing there, taking on this animal as it bit into my thigh, I had a sudden and terrifying realization of what I was dealing with. My entire front side was exposed to an attacking grizzly, and I knew that would be trouble if I couldn't get out of the way. I glanced to the left and saw some bushes off the trail. In an awkward, backward two-step, I hurled myself off the trail into those bushes that would surely be a lot softer than the hardness of the teeth buried in my thigh.

I landed somewhat on my side and back and quickly looked around me. Instantly, it was peaceful and nothing was coming at me, trying to tear my leg apart. *"But Jenna,"* came my next flash of thought— *"She is back on the trail. The bear is on the trail. She needs to come down here!"*

I yelled, "Jenna, come down here! Jump off the trail into the bushes!"

Jenna never heard me, but the bear did.

Out of my left eye I could see THE BEAR. It somehow was climbing onto the trail, and when I had yelled and moved, it turned its attention to me.

The bear turned its head quickly to the left and looked at me, and I have never seen anything move that fast in my life. It was back engaged with me, on top of me in a flash. I had barely enough time to get into the fetal position and protect my vulnerable front side. The bear started pulling and lifting me up by my back pack. She made no contact with my body as she thrashed me around. I kept protecting the back of my neck with my hands, but while this was happening, a totally different realization set in: *"I am the one with the backpack. Jenna has nothing on her back. If this animal does to her back what it is doing to my back pack, it will tear her apart and she will be dead!"*

I needed to keep this bear with me and take it away from Jenna.

"Stay with me" became my motto. Somehow I turned away from the bear and rolled to the right—only to plunge down the face of the mountain pass, a thirty-foot sheer drop.

It felt strangely good for a moment to be falling and not having something heavy on top of me. Even the landing did not hurt.

My second fall—the thirty-foot drop. This time with a bear in tow.

While falling, I had instinctively kept my eyes closed as a protective mechanism. (To be more precise, my right eye was bloody and already closed, but my left eye joined it in the closed position.)

Once I landed I found myself on my back. My left eye opened, and in my right hand was…a bear! Somehow I must have grabbed the bear to pull it down with me and away from Jenna. But what do you do when you find yourself on a narrow mountain shelf with a bear in your right hand?

The scruff of the bear's neck was very thick, much more so than the scruff of a dog's neck.

"Maybe I can hit it in the face with a rock," I think.

My left hand was grasping around me but all I could feel was shale—crumbly, useless material that disintegrated in my hand and would certainly not deter this bear. It would probably piss it off even more if I threw shale into its face.

In the meantime, two hazel-brown eyes with small black pupils were staring at me. I could sense no anger or fear or any emotion whatsoever in those eyes.

All I could see was determination to eliminate me.

When I realized I would not find a rock big enough to fight the bear, I somehow ripped myself loose from its weight and turned back onto my stomach again, with my hands behind my neck. The bear was furious and started to attack me with a vengeance. It was biting into my hands and head, and clawing into my neck and skull. I could hear bones crack as if I was cracking my knuckles or popping my back, but the sense of pressure was deeper, and there certainly was no pain or tension release happening. This sensation was something I had never felt before.

Nevertheless, I was determined to stay put. As long as this animal was with me it was OK—because it wasn't with Jenna. I hoped that Jenna had had enough time to run away and down the trail to go look for help.

Strange thoughts swam around in my head: Maybe I was an actor and they were filming a scene for a movie in which my character was being attacked by an animal. Or maybe I was the stunt double? But don't they keep the stunt double safe as well? *"Hey, production crew! I'm getting beat up here!"*

Man, this attack just kept going.

I was kind of getting tired of it by now.

I slowly started to drift off.

Is this what an out-of-body experience is like? It seemed as if I was watching myself from a distance— from the director's chair, actually. Only I was the director as well as the stunt-double. It was a weird scene to watch and I wasn't sure what to do.

This was not going the way I expected it to go as the director, since I had never directed a movie in my life. Yet I felt paralyzed in regard to what to do next…

…until suddenly I felt a much closer crack. And then another.

I came back from la-la land and was suddenly 110 percent aware and in the moment.

I realized, *"If I keep playing dead, I actually will be dead in a few moments!"*

What help would I be to Jenna at that point? *I think I have kept this animal busy long enough to give Jenna time to get away. Now I need to think about myself.*

After the second crack and bite into my skull, I could feel the bear's bottom incisor going into my skull bone. I ripped myself loose from her jaw and rolled and tumbled another twenty-five feet further down the rocky cliffside. My feet landed solidly on a ledge. My back was resting against the mountain in a crevice with a tiny little creek created by the snow melt from the day before. That water was cold and it was getting me all wet. What a mess.

I was pissed off at this point and was ready to push the bear off the mountain if it came for me again. There were no other ledges left below me. That fall would be certain death—for the bear, I hoped.

The bear looked down at me from over the edge above and walked away. Suddenly I was alone.

How weird.

And then I heard a scream…

For a parent, the worst thing you can possibly hear is your child screaming, full of fear and mental pain, and to be unable to do anything about it. Jenna's scream was the worst sound I had ever heard.

Then there was silence.

The bear got to Jenna after all.

I had hoped I had kept it busy long enough. I was wrong.

What a failure I was.

From their initial place of emotional anguish, my thoughts fought back to a place of reason.

I did not want to cry out and anger the animal even more, and I needed to assess my wounds. Strings from my scalp were hanging in front of my face. My right eye was closed. I moved a scalp string out of the way and felt my right cheek to see if my eyeball was hanging out. *Ok, no eyeball here.* So I slowly moved my hand, carefully feeling my cheek, which was crusted with blood up to my eye. I could feel the eyelid was closed and I opened it with my left hand. I could see Grinnell Lake. *Great, my right eye is still there and I can see out of it, and the rest can be fixed by surgery.* And by the way, Grinnell Lake is still the prettiest blue lake I have ever seen.

Next, I wanted to know what was up with my skull so I slowly felt my way up to my forehead. I felt bone. All the way to the top of my head there was bone. It felt as if my scalp had been crunched together into my neck. Dr. Johan the diagnostician stepped in again. "*They can easily just pull that forwards, a couple of stitches and it will be like new. Oh, look at these wounds in my arm. You can actually see the tendons move; that is so interesting. Once a physical therapist, always a physical therapist,*" I thought.

Time to get back to reality and yell for Jenna. I had heard nothing while I was assessing my wounds.

"Jenna!" I called.

"Dad!" I heard.

It was the best sound I'd ever heard.

That *"Dad!"* was strong and full of life.

She is alive; I am ecstatic!

"How are your eyes?" I yelled out. Why so specific? I think I was projecting my injuries onto her.

"They are fine," she yelled back. "I got hurt, but I am OK!"

"It got me kinda bad," I yelled back.

The next thing I did was yell, "Help!"

That was the extent of the discussion around our injuries. Jenna and I were both torn up, but neither one of us wanted to worry the other, so we kept that information to ourselves. Jenna joined in with my calls for help, and for the next few minutes that is all we did. In the meantime the stream along my back was getting uncomfortably cold. I needed to get out of this situation.

In one of those *Bear Attacks of the Century* books that I had picked up in the gift shop and read the night before, there had been a story about a woman in Alaska who had been attacked and mauled by a black bear. In order to protect her damaged scalp, she had pulled the cap of her jacket over her head. *"That is something I need to do,"* I thought, *"because I must look horrible and can't have anyone see my head like this."* I took my backpack off and retrieved my jacket. I placed the nylon cap of the jacket over my skull with the jacket hanging on my back.

"I have to crawl up to the ledge," I thought. *"I need to go find Jenna."*

I reminded myself to take the camera off my neck where it was still dangling and left my backpack off as well. Just like they say, in case of an airplane emergency landing, leave all your stuff behind; it is not as important as you are, so get yourself to safety first.

Ugh. I was a bit stiff. It was hard to move myself out of this position but somehow I managed to crawl back on top of the ledge. I stood up and felt a bit woozy. *Maybe I should just stay put.*

Then I remembered a polar expedition management game I had just played. My employer, Scripps Health in San Diego, had sent me to the Advisory Board Fellowship in Washington, DC, which is leadership training for health care managers and executives. I had lost that game because I was one of the survivors who decided to go get help, only to end up terribly lost. *"Stay put and people will find you,"* I remembered, was the lesson of that exercise. So I lay down and tried to stay comfortable and stay away from the edge just in case I passed out.

I resumed my yelling for help.

For the next forty-five minutes or so, Jenna and I kept yelling *"Help!"*

We alternated our yelling. I kept my mind busy by making sure the strength in Jenna's voice did not go down, but she sounded as strong as the first yell. Apparently the guided hikers had just arrived at the drop-off point on one of the lower lakes in the valley because Jenna yelled, "Dad, I see people coming our way—a large group. They just got off the boat." That was great news because this yelling for help was taking a bit longer than I expected.

But before the large group of hikers reached us, other people arrived.

"There's someone here!" Jenna suddenly yelled to me.

"Finally!" I thought, because next to getting tired of yelling for help I was getting cold and thirsty as well. A couple who was hiking ahead of the naturalist-led group had heard some commotion earlier.

Much later, after Jenna and I were healed, they told us they did not know if they had heard the actual attack in progress, but at the time they started to hear what they thought were birds. But as they got nearer they soon realized that it sounded like someone calling for help. They needed to investigate.

They reached Jenna first, who cautioned them to be careful just in case she was still around.

"She," indeed: Our attacker was a mother grizzly trying to protect two cubs. At the time, I had no idea. I'd been under the impression that this was a bear we just literally bumped into who reacted with aggression to defend itself, but a mother grizzly is a different story. When Jenna had made the turn around the large rock that stuck out into the trail, she had seen two little cubs and a big mama bear, right in front of her. The bear had no idea what was approaching her and Jenna noted that the bear looked up in surprise much in the same way Jenna must have done. Jenna's response was actually immediate and swift. She stepped back very quickly and yelled, which allowed me time to step in front of her to protect her.

What a strange situation the bear and I were in. Here were two parents, trying to protect their young, both willing to sacrifice their own lives, and we made that decision without deliberation. Something much more primitive was at work.

Strangely, it felt good to me that I had stuck with the fight versus having a flight response. Wow, who would have thought that I, the guy nearly always picked last in gym class, would actually stand up to a grizzly bear and give it quite a run!

CHAPTER 5 57

Our unused bear spray, including some blood stains

The first person I saw after Jenna yelled that help had arrived was a guy who slid down into some bushes right above me. His eyes opened wide, and he looked at me in a way I will never forget.

"I must look really bad," I thought.

He asked how I was, and I asked how Jenna was, but all I remember hearing was that help was on the way.

And then he asked what he could do to make me more comfortable. Suddenly things became less acute. I could let go of my need to stay in the moment—alert and present for Jenna—and think about myself.

By this time more hikers had arrived to offer assistance: Two young guys who I remember vividly wore beanies on their heads. People on the trail above me threw down their jackets and sweaters to place under my head and neck so that I could cushion myself from the hardness of the rocky ground. I asked people if they were sure they wanted to lend me their sweaters since they would get dirty with my blood. I recall folks looked at me strangely when I asked that, or when I apologized for them having to help me. *"Don't worry about it,"* was the general reply.

I wanted my camera back for some reason, and the two guys were able to retrieve my backpack and my camera and give me a bottle of the fruity water that I had brought along for the hike. I was getting more thirsty and colder by the minute. Two young ladies, probably in their early twenties, arrived on the scene. They took the lead in making Jenna and myself comfortable. It seemed to come very natural to them.

I constantly asked how Jenna was, and these fine folks kept assuring me that she was doing fine. I began to shiver. Somehow knowing that Jenna was OK and relaxing a bit seemed to be making my situation worse. No longer did I have that parental protective mechanism going on; slowly I became less and less alert. The adrenaline rush was going away.

Everyone wanted me to stay awake and stay on my back but I was too uncomfortable with that rock sticking into my neck. I asked people to help me up. *"No, you need to stay still until medical help arrives,"* they said.

If only they knew how correct they were.

But I *stubbornly* told them, "Either you help me or I get up myself," so they reluctantly yet patiently and skillfully helped me up.

It is amazing what people will do for another human in need. I started to get colder even with loads of jackets on me. Finally one of the young women covered my body with hers. I asked her, "Are you sure you want to do that? You are going to get all dirty," but she said yes, calmly and firmly, that she could keep me warmer and protected from the wind that way. That human touch—not just the physical warmth but also the emotional warmth of another person caring—was what I needed at that point. I shivered less and calmed down a bit more, which undoubtedly kept me alive and in the moment.

The area where the attack occurred

— CHAPTER 6 —

The Rescue

Almost two hours later, a rescue crew arrived. Unbeknownst to Jenna and me, the first couple who found us had split up after they realized what had happened. The woman was a runner and had run down the mountain to alert the ranger leading the large group of hikers. That ranger had a walkie-talkie and had radioed down to the Many Glacier Hotel to report that people had been attacked by a bear. Forty-five minutes after the attack, the Grinnell Trail had been shut down, and at least sixty people were now on a closed trail, unable to proceed until we were removed from the mountain. Rangers were being contacted and the rescue system had gone into full alert.

DANGER
8-25-05 10:00 am

This Trail Is Closed
Because of Bear Danger

Entering a closed area or removal of
this sign is punishable by fine up to
$500 or imprisonment for 6 months, or both.

Sign posted at the beginning of Grinnell Trail once word had come down the mountain of our attack

Gary Moses was the park ranger in charge that day and as it turned out was the park's bear expert as well.

Katie, one of the younger rangers in the park, was part of his team. These two people ended up being the two who interacted with me the most. I mean that in a literal sense, because when they arrived at my side and asked others to take a backseat, they were positioned to the left of my face and right above it. I now had to trust these new people, and the two girls who had initially taken the "first responder" rescue lead had to take a backseat, which of course they did.

I work in the health care industry; oftentimes I've found myself in situations where a handoff does not happen very well, which leads to upset and confused people. Ultimately, the patient suffers. On the side of a mountain on August 25, 2005, none of that happened. A better patient handoff could not possibly have occurred.

"How is Jenna?" was my first question to these official-looking and -acting people.

"She is going to be fine and we are here to focus on you."

I am sure that I asked about Jenna a few more times, but here events start to get a little bit more blurred. Other rangers arrived as well and they all started to slowly assess me and ask me what happened. I explained and told them how I tried to keep the bear with me and that I had fallen three times and crawled back up again once. There was no more sitting up to be done at this point though. They stabilized my neck, started to explore my wounds and inserted an IV to put some fluids back into me as they continuously monitored my blood pressure and pulse. We talked about some mundane stuff, and I was so thankful to them and made sure to thank them over and over again.

The assessment continued to my legs, and a more mature female ranger started to take off my shorts.

"Wait!" I yelled.

"What, are we hurting you?" she and another ranger asked in a very caring manner.

"No, no not at all, but have you guys ever watched Seinfeld?"

I got some confirming but confused responses.

"OK," I said, "So listen, there is this one episode. George comes out of a cold shower, and a female spots his frontal nudity. Now he is trying to explain himself this entire episode. It's about shrinkage. It's cold up here and I want no assessments of that sort when you pull my shorts off."

That broke the ice, so to speak, and everyone laughed.

We needed laughter at that time and it made me feel a bit more like myself.

(Luckily I had listened to my mother all those years and I did put on clean underwear before we started hiking. Gary told me later that they've talked about me joking around for years afterward; apparently it really was a funny moment.)

The more fluid Gary pushed into me, the more leaks I sprung. I had so many wounds, yet because I was dehydrated, these wounds had not previously leaked body fluids. Eventually, that changed, but my blood pressure was dropping and becoming very hard to find any more and we were kind of in limbo. The situation was obviously not getting much better.

Gary told me later that when he sat next to me he was on the edge of the cliff. There was no room left behind him.

Katie, the young ranger positioned at my head, started to cry. Gary tried to comfort her and so did I. She could obviously see that this was a dire situation and that I possibly would not make it, but I did not feel that way and told her that I would be fine. I may have been slightly delirious, but I liked the fact that she cried. That, together with the joking, humanized this surreal experience. It also allowed me the opportunity to be me and switch into my preferred mode—to care for someone other than myself at that point. I thought it was wonderful that she cried.

A rather large helicopter had passed overhead about an hour or so after Gary had arrived on the scene. "That is the sound of your rescue," he had said, but that rescue sure seemed to be taking a long time.

Of course, I didn't know it, but a different rescue team located seventy feet above us on the trail was trying to find a way to attach ropes to the rocks and boulders so they could lift me up from off the ledge. Unfortunately, this team was unable to find solid rock that was stable enough to attach hooks to in order to hoist us up.

The whirring sound of "our rescue" had not returned, and I could see that Gary was getting a bit restless. He had made the call for a helicopter rescue after he had assessed the situation, but he knew that rescue teams were reticent to do helicopter short-haul rescues because of the possible dangers involved. Earlier that year, a helicopter had crashed on Mount Rainier during a short-haul rescue mission and there was a movement afoot to restrict any more such operations on federal lands. Luckily, Gary knew the gravity of our situation and he saved our lives by convincing the team a short-haul helicopter rescue was worth the risk. As it turned out, my neck was badly broken in many spots, the most crucial break being at Cervical 1-2 level. Any other method of rescue could have—probably would have—killed me.

At Glacier National Park, there are two different options for helicopter assistance. One is provided by a commercial outlet that does scenic tours around the park. Their helicopters are rather large and are not easily landed or maneuvered into tight spaces. These folks had brought the rangers to us. The other system is based at Kalispell Medical Center. It is one of the only such rescue systems owned by a hospital in the country. This helicopter team is called the A.L.E.R.T. team, which stands for Advanced Life Support and Emergency Rescue Team. This team includes professional pilots, nurses specifically trained for trauma, and other technical personnel, all focused on responding quickly in situations when time is life.

That day the team had been activated to transport a patient from Browning, on the east side of the divide, to Kalispell, on the west side of the divide. Their delay was certainly felt on the mountainside where Jenna was stable, but I was slowly starting to slip into a worse and worse shock situation.

CHAPTER 6

The A.L.E.R.T. helicopter preparing to haul us off the mountain. This landing site is right off the road between the Many Glaciers Hotel and the Swiftcurrent Lodge.

Suddenly a whirring sound became evident, and Gary said the helicopter was back. I could certainly distinguish the difference between the two helicopters and Gary explained what was going to happen. He told me that a stretcher would be lowered down to me. I would be securely strapped into the stretcher with a paramedic positioned right next to me.

Gary became more animated as he signaled coordinates to the helicopter pilot who was now hovering above us. A man attached to a long rope was being lowered down to the ledge. (Later on, when I thanked the man, he referred to himself as the "dope on the rope.")

Gary and Katie ensured that I was secured on top of the stretcher and immobilized. "You are going to have the view of your life," Gary told me as he strapped me in.

Jenna and I had not planned a scenic helicopter tour of Glacier for this trip since that would have been too expensive for us, but in my current state, I figured we may as well make the best of the situation, and I was looking forward to the trip from the mountain side to a waiting ambulance down the valley.

Our positions on the ledge about fifty-to-sixty feet under the trail

Gary began motioning to the helicopter, and slowly but surely I was going up. The "dope on the rope," a rather stoic, mustached man in his fifties, told me that he was there to take care of me. There was nothing scary about the flight, and while being lifted I gave in to any resistance I might have had and just let people help me. The wind gently crossed my face while we were flying down the valley.

Sadly, the great view Gary mentioned never materialized. All I could see was the guy above me on the rope.

CHAPTER 6 67

My view under the helicopter

▶ The View from Above: Ken Justus, Rescue Helicopter Pilot

August 25th, 2005 was another beautiful summer day in Northwest Montana. I was at the Blackfeet Hospital in Browning when we heard about it: a double bear mauling on Grinnell Glacier trail. Glacier National Park Service was requesting a "short-haul" rescue; that's a situation in which a patient needs to be rescued from a place where there is no safe area to land the helicopter nearby. I had been approved to do these kinds of rescues just two months prior.

In a short-haul rescue, the paramedic is lowered to the patient via a longline from the helicopter, and then the patient and paramedic are flown out together, secured to the end of this line, to a suitable landing zone where they can actually be loaded into the helicopter. (Preferably as short a distance as possible to reduce the risk, hence the name "short-haul") The A.L.E.R.T. program which I had become a part of in 2003 had adopted this technique from the National Parks of Canada.

We first had to take a cardiac patient from Browning back to Kalispell and then pick up our gear at the hangar. On the flight, I was a little apprehensive. The only "live" person I had ever had on the line before was for training. There's a special patch for our flight suits that only crews who respond to bear maulings wear; I didn't have one yet. It was a little overwhelming to be responding to my first short-haul rescue as well as my first bear mauling at the same time.

Back in Kalispell, we transferred our patient and then quickly but methodically grabbed all our gear: a 150-foot Kevlar logging line, flying litter, special helmet and radio, some safety devices to keep the longline from being accidently jettisoned. It was about a twenty-minute flight to Many Glacier, but we knew they had been waiting, so it couldn't go quickly enough. As we passed west Glacier, we called Park Dispatch and they gave us the call number of the ranger to contact on scene. We then made a beeline thru the notch at Grinnell Overlook. I remembered that my parents were hiking in the area and I was hoping and praying that it wasn't them.

We flew past the incident to do a "face-to-face" with park rangers at Keyhole in Many Glacier. Keyhole is a landing zone just off the main road across Swiftcurrent Lake from the Lodge. It is cut out of the trees and from the air it looks like a keyhole.

After landing and shutting down, we were asked to go back up and have a look to see if we would be able to operate so close to the cliff. We jumped back in, fired up and had a look. I was relieved to see that there were no trees nearby that I would have to thread the line through. There was also plenty of clearance from the cliff because it sidesteps as it goes up. I was confident that I would be able to pull them off the ledge they were on. The hard part was going to be setting the medic down there!

We returned to Keyhole to set up our gear and put the medic, Jerry Anderson, on the end of the rope. We had to shut down again to make sure we weren't rushed and got everything right. It all went fairly quickly, but I was sure for the people involved that it wasn't going quickly enough.

Within ten minutes I had Jerry on the end of the line and was giving him an awesome ride up over Lake Josephine and over the trail toward the site. Just as we were approaching the ledge, I lost communication with Jerry for some reason and had to talk with the ranger, Gary Moses, to help determine the height above the ground for my medic, as I couldn't see his shadow until we got right over the narrow ledge. At that point, it was time to set him down without banging him against the next cliff wall. It went smoothly and I was relieved.

Jerry unhooked himself and the flying litter and I backed away to decrease the rotor wash and noise to the area. A little while later I got a call that they were ready for pickup. Jerry didn't mess around! And I'm sure Gary had Johan ready.

I brought the line to Jerry and he hooked himself and the flying litter to it and gave me the thumbs up as Gary also called to say that they were ready. I knew if I was over the cliff that as soon as I lifted them they would swing clear, so that was my plan. It worked out well. Had to keep the airspeed down below about 40 knots or the litter would spin like crazy, so it was a slow smooth flight back to Keyhole.

I realized that the landing zone was paved, so I needed to be really smooth setting them down there. Luckily the sun was shining and I was able to see the shadow as we got over the area and made a smooth touchdown. I also had to leave enough room for the helicopter to land, so I landed them forward, toward the waiting ambulance. I then landed behind them, making sure not to land on the rope.

By the time I got the helicopter shut down, they already had Johan loaded into the Babb Ambulance, so I didn't get to see him. Travis Willcut, the flight nurse, went into the ambulance with Johan and Jerry and I went back up for round two, which went better than round one.

Jerry had gotten the radio problem fixed and we were able to communicate. By then I had learned that the patients were a father and daughter, so I had ruled out this being my parents. As we lifted Jenna off the ledge, Gary came over the radio and said something about us (A.L.E.R.T.) being "miracle workers" and I could sense his relief.

After landing for the fourth time that day at Keyhole, I shut down and reconfigured the helicopter to carry a patient. I remember sensing gratitude from Jenna's eyes as she was unloaded. We then loaded Johan into the helicopter and Jenna went to the ambulance. I also remember them having some kind of tender banter during this time although they probably couldn't see each other. I have two daughters and was thinking I would want them rescued first, but I was sure they knew what they were doing. Always take out the most critical first. And from what I could see of Johan, he was a mess!

It was twenty minutes back to the ER in Kalispell, then hot refuel and back for Jenna. By the time we had her at the ER about an hour after Johan, they were already talking about sending him on to Seattle in our fixed-wing aircraft, A.L.E.R.T. 2. I remember thinking that it was too bad they were going to be separated.

After putting all the gear away, I called my boss and told him about the excitement and to expect to see us on the news. One of the local new stations came by and interviewed me by the helicopter. I hate that stuff.

I felt that I should go see Jenna since she was separated from her dad, but never did, which later I regretted. Normally we have very little interaction with a patient after they get to the hospital. It's not the norm to visit people we don't know, but little did I know how close we were to become in the future. I saw Johan and Jenna on national television over the next couple weeks, but we didn't meet personally until April, when the hospital brought them up for our annual fundraiser banquet. Johan told me then that he was going to come back on the one-year anniversary and do that hike again.

I wasn't really interested; I knew there would be more media hoopla than hiking, so I didn't go along that day. But I did bump into him on the Hidden Lake Overlook trail the next day after a friend and I climbed Mount Canon and Clements Mountain. He invited me to go on another hike with him, which I did, and we have become close hiking buddies ever since. Our friendship is centered around hiking in Glacier National Park every year for one week, but extends to every month as we talk about last year's adventure and the next year's plans. We have covered hundreds of miles together, sometimes a hundred miles in five days. We've slept in tents and cabins together, fished many gorgeous lakes, canoed for miles, sat around campfires, ate great meals of fresh-caught trout, drank a few fine beers, gorged on assorted berries along the trail, enjoyed pastries and each other's company in Polebridge (while it poured down rain just after Ranger Emmerich informed us that the park was closed due to the government shutdown).

We've even seen a few bears—but none close.

Up In the Air, Hanging by a Thread

We quickly arrived down in the valley, and very gently I was lowered to the ground. This helicopter transfer was memorable for its gentleness (unlike some of the gurney-to-bed transfers I was to experience during my long hospital stays).

I was transferred to a waiting ambulance, which offered the first real warmth I had felt since being taken off the mountain. The nurse at the foot of my gurney was very comforting and was the first person all day who did not give me the "Oh-My-God" look. She calmed me by her presence and by keeping me posted about what was happening to Jenna.

The team asked if I minded a short delay in my arrival at a hospital so they could get Jenna from the ledge first. Did I mind? "Of course not!" I didn't care that much about myself, but please, go get Jenna. I didn't want her to spend any more time on that mountain than necessary.

The team recovered Jenna from the ledge quickly (or at least it seemed that way to me). Before I knew it, the helicopter was back and I was moved out of the ambulance and the crew let me say something to Jenna before they flew me to the hospital.

"Jenna, make sure when you call Mom that she gets the call from you, OK? I don't want a hospital person calling, because that would just freak her out."

Jenna told me she would call personally, and we wished each other well before I was loaded back into the helicopter. I have no memory of flying to Kalispell Medical Center except that I was still looking forward to that great view that I never got when I was hanging below the helicopter.

I still did not get that view.

— CHAPTER 7 —
Life, Reset

Before I knew it, I was being wheeled into the Emergency Room (ER). It was white, it was clean, there were lots of good-looking young people, and they all were so competent.

I hadn't died and gone to heaven; I was still alive and had gone to heaven-on-earth. The cleanliness and professionalism of the health care professionals at Kalispell was amazing to me as they slowly removed blood and dirt-stained clothing from my body—whatever was left of both my clothing *and* my body...

They asked if they could take pictures of me. "Sure," I said, getting ready to smile for the camera, but I just saw a person taking pictures of my injuries, not my face as in a normal snapshot. They later would send the pictures to me, and it was quite a shock to see what I had looked like for the first time.

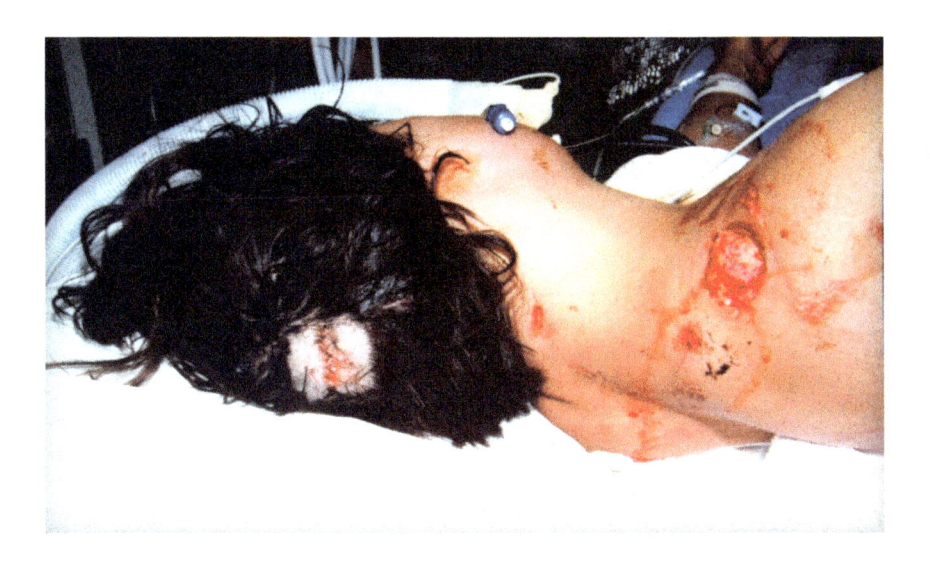

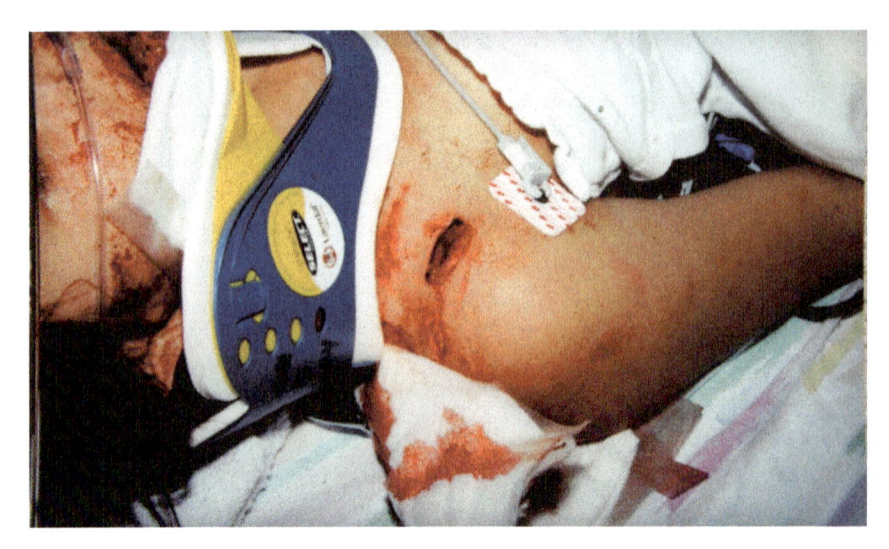

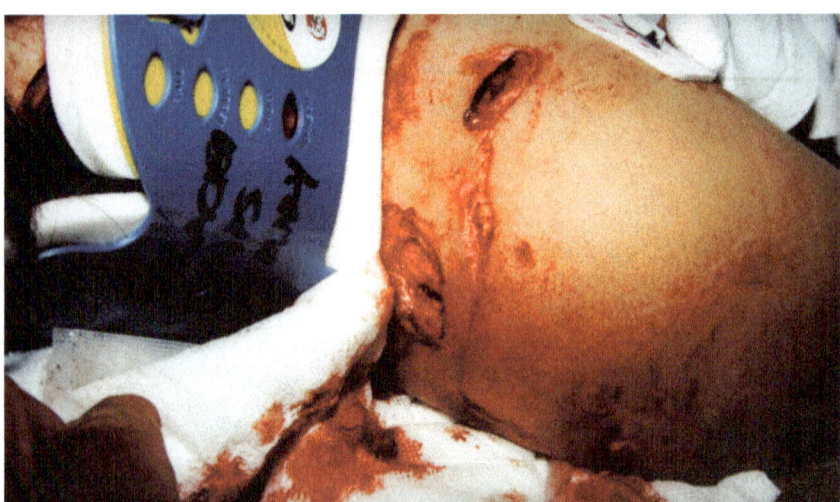

Jenna's injury pictures from the Kalispell Medical Center ER: visible are the lacerated mouth corner, bite and claw wounds on her head and some going into the right shoulder joint. Not visible are the fractured thoracic vertebra and sacrum and a lacerated posterior ankle.

CHAPTER 7   75

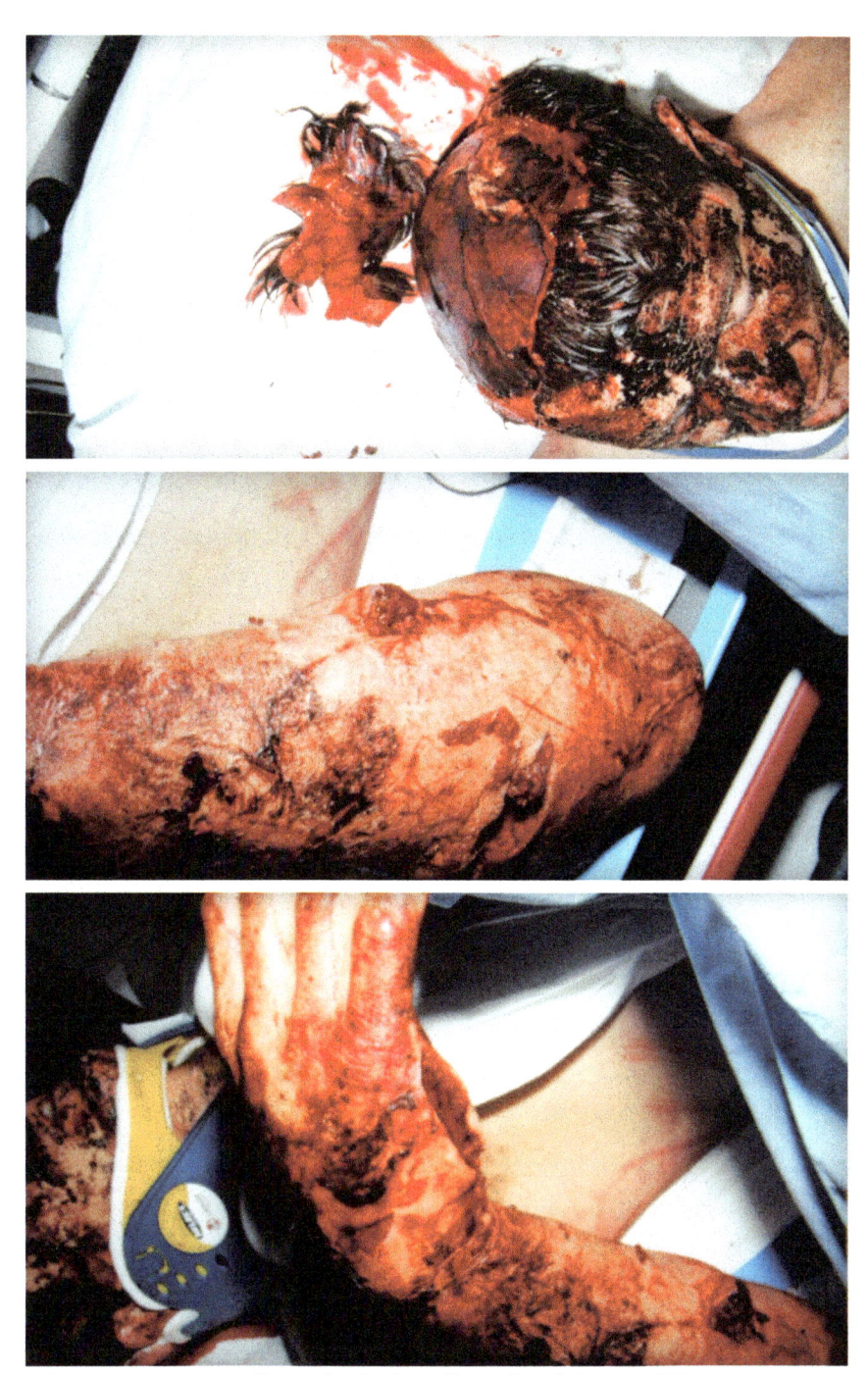

My injury pictures from the Kalispell Medical Center ER

The entire staff seemed to work in such great unison that I couldn't distinguish a tech from a nurse or a doctor. They all knew what to do and that was all that mattered. They were very attentive, responding to every "ooh," I uttered with, "Does it hurt?"

Invariably I would reply, "No, but I like to make noise so I can anticipate the pain. If it doesn't come, then that's great." It was my little stress relief mind game.

Another thing the staff told me later was I continuously thanked them. One of the physicians said I was the most thankful patient she had ever had. What she didn't know was that on the mountain, right after the attack, I had thanked God for keeping me alive, along with important people in my life that had recently passed away, like my longtime patient, Sophie Brodie, and of course my parents and my father-in-law. So yes, I was very thankful. I kept thanking everyone, everywhere I went.

A CT scan had to be taken, so that was performed. I was cleaned as much as possible and bandages were applied all over my body. I kind of felt like a mummy, but a clean mummy that was finally warm and still alive!

The staff explained to me that because of the extent of my injuries, I had to be flown to Seattle. (I had never been to Seattle so I remember being excited. I still had not realized how badly hurt I was—that I still might have to fight for my life—and that this was no longer vacation.)

The staff asked me if I had a physician back in San Diego. What I heard was, "Do you have a trauma surgeon in San Diego?" That was because I did know an amazing one.

During the second phase of the attack, when the bear was lifting me up by my backpack, I remembered thinking, "Wow, this will make a great story back home at the system-wide management meetings." In 2005, as it turned out, I was in charge of proposing agenda items for this meeting—more than 500 managers, directors and executives from more than thirty sites across San Diego County. This responsibility was mine as a graduate of an internal Scripps Health management development initiative called Leadership Academy, although one of our senior executives called the final shots. But maybe this time, with a real-live bear attack, I would have an agenda item that would make the cut!

So when I thought I heard, "Do you have a trauma surgeon?" I said, "Yes, and his name is Brent Eastman. He is in charge of the doctors at Scripps, and he knows me, and you need to call him."

I had spoken to Dr. Eastman prior to the graduation trip because he was from Jackson, Wyoming. I had let him know Jenna and I would visit his hometown, hike a little, and then proceed to Glacier. He urged me to stay longer at Jackson Hole and joked a bit with me about that. I can imagine he was a bit surprised when he got a call from an emergency room in Kalispell.

Dr. Eastman recalls that he spoke to the Kalispell physician, Dr. Lawrence Iwersen, and then tried to offer some advice. Dr. Iwersen is an expert on grizzly bear attacks and told Dr. Eastman with wonderful Montana honesty; "With all due respect, Dr. Eastman, how many grizzly bear attacks do you take care of in San Diego?"

Point well taken, of course.

Dr. Eastman is a great gentleman and also quite an expert physician in the setup and operation of trauma systems. He had been instrumental in creating or consulting on many trauma systems all over the country. If I had to suffer such a massive injury, I could not have picked a better place to have it. The WAMI (Washington, Alaska, Montana, Idaho) trauma system district is huge and covers four states. After being stabilized in the field, people injured inside this district are transported expeditiously to a facility that offers the appropriate level of care.

In our case, I had to be flown to the region's trauma center with the levels of care required for me, but Jenna was able to stay in Kalispell. Trauma systems save many lives because emergency procedures for different types of injuries have been previously established. These procedures include appropriate placement for the patient, and time it will take to fly a patient from one facility to another.

My flight time to Seattle would be about ninety minutes.

After my wonderful experience at Kalispell Medical Center, I was loaded into a fixed-wing plane and flown to Seattle. *"Again, no view,"*

I thought, and for a person who always likes to sit next to the window that should have been quite a bummer. But I did not care about that at this time. Once I was placed in the fixed wing plane I was told that I had severely fractured my neck. They gave me the specifics; I had sustained a compound fracture of C2 (the second cervical vertebra) and several other fractures, including some ribs.

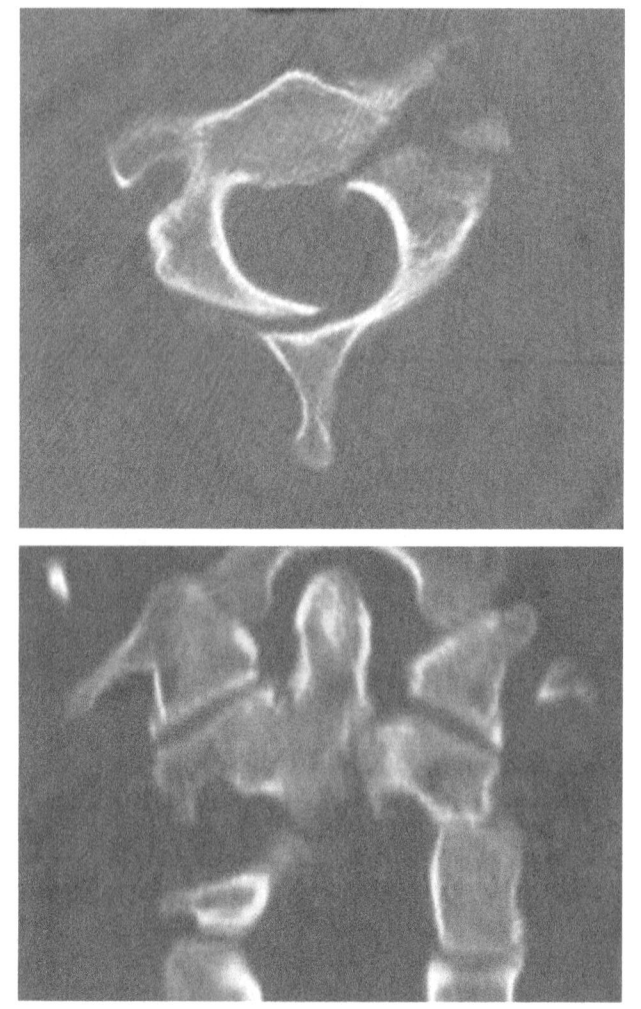

Two images of my second vertebra and its multiple fractures. Being alive and well after this is a miracle.

Now I knew what that "rock" that had been stabbing me in the back of my head on the mountain had been. I had probably felt my own fracture; and yes, I had heard cracks in the lower part of my neck, so I was not surprised something was broken. But a compound fracture of C2 was serious.

"I want a halo (a medical device used to stabilize the cervical spine after traumatic injuries). I don't want a fusion," I remember saying vehemently.

As a physical therapist, I knew that a cervical fusion could dramatically limit my neck motion, and I wanted to be able to return to as close to normal as possible. I imagine the staff in the plane were amazed that I was so cognizant and knowledgeable about the severity and treatment of my injuries.

The flight seemed short, probably due to the pain medication I'd received. Actually, I do not recall having any major pain prior to the medication being given, but as a professional, I know that pain can (and will) develop later.

Arriving in Seattle was a blur. Fast-moving people, equipment, and sounds. I assumed these people knew what they were doing. They sure acted like it. I did have a feeling of slight disappointment with my arrival in Seattle. It was irrational, to be sure, but I was disappointed I would not get to see much of the city; critically wounded, but all I could think about was that I wanted to see the sights—especially that place where they throw the fish around—Pike's Place.

"We are going to clean you up in surgery." I didn't know who said that, but *whatever; I am in your hands and everything seems to be working OK, so do whatever you need to do to fix me up again.*

I kept up that philosophy. All these bodily damages should easily be fixed with a little surgery. "Just make sure you do not do surgery to my neck because I want a halo," I kept thinking—maybe even saying.

Unconscious and conscious worlds started to blur together. *Lights, camera, action* is what it seemed like to me, and I was back on the mountain again, thinking I was a stunt man in some Grizzly Adams movie that nobody realized was real. Or was all of this a dream? I did not know anymore.

The "little" surgery I was anticipating ended up taking seven hours, followed up a few days later by a ten-hour marathon session of several surgeries all rolled into one.

My head had to be cleaned and covered to prevent infection. Between 60 and 80 percent of my scalp was gone, and the wound was down to the bone. Two arteries that run in that area had been torn off, but the jacket that I had covered my head with had sealed those wounds very well, which had kept me from bleeding to death.

The hole in my right forearm had torn tendons that needed repairing.

A claw that had penetrated my eye socket had torn a muscle and caused a fracture of the wall of the eye socket.

Those were just the injuries above the neck.

Below the neck, I had more than twenty wounds large enough to need serious care. Dirt was everywhere, and they were slathered in bear slime. Turns out that bears carry at least twenty-five exotic-type bacteria in their mouths, and all those bugs thrive in an environment of low or no oxygen. That meant the normal method of closing wounds was not an option. My wounds needed to stay open so the bear's mouth bacteria would not have an opportunity to proliferate.

I had been treated in Kalispell by the world's foremost expert on grizzly-bear-inflicted wounds, so I arrived in Seattle with the best possible instructions.

Back home in Escondido, Marilyn had been notified of the attack in a very professional way by Kalispell Medical Center. They had Jenna explain to her what had happened so that she could hear her voice and be reassured.

Marilyn made lightning-fast arrangements the same afternoon to get her brother-in-law to Jenna at Kalispell and pick up my car, and to get to me in Seattle. Meanwhile my sister-in-law, Denise, would stay with Stephanie, our younger daughter, who now had to hold down the fort and take care of the yard and all the animals.

That by itself was a huge task. I had approximately 300 birds at the time. Luckily most of the yard was on automatic irrigation, but the animal care was quite a job for a young girl just starting her junior year in high school. How they all stayed so calm and organized is still amazing to me; what is even more amazing is the response from everyone around us.

▶ Caring for the Birds

Any time I go away for more than two days, I need someone to take care of my menagerie of birds. Although Stephanie stepped in to take care of the birds while I was hospitalized in Seattle, once the news was out that I had been attacked, an entire army of bird friends descended on our property.

I belong to a hobbyist bird club called the North County Aviculturists (NCA) and friends from the club leaped in to help after my accident. They actually did a more thorough job of bird care than I often do. I tolerate quite bit of chaos and mess around my aviaries, but every time my birdsitters took care of my birds they would sanitize food dishes and water bowls, clean and organize other things, etc. They were just awesome.

Many others in the bird club also stepped up to do whatever else was necessary to help out. In no time at all, bowls had been changed out, bushes were trimmed and cages better organized. Nothing had even a whisper of a chance to become disorganized while I was hospitalized.

I found out later that at one point, my bird club friends were even talking about bringing in a tractor to make the bird area wheelchair accessible. Luckily, there was no need for that, but don't ever think my bird friends don't know what they are doing.

Once I came back home, I was not initially able to fully take care of my birds with my halo on, but I did a little. One thing I could not do was travel to purchase birdseed, but just like the moms from the dance team organized meals, the ladies from our bird club collected funds to cover birdseed, bought the seed and made sure everything was taken care of. You don't realize how many friends you have until you really need them, and I have so many.

The Word Spreads Back Home

By this time, news of the attack was just hitting the media. Several people at my employer, Scripps Health, were already rallying the troops, so to speak.

After his initial conversation with Dr. Iwersen in Kalispell, Dr. Eastman had informed the CEO of Scripps Health, Chris Van Gorder, that I'd been injured, so that the hospital could be prepared for my arrival back at my "home hospital." Meanwhile, once Marilyn was settled in Seattle, she called my boss, Mary Jo Webb, who promptly asked Dr. Eastman to do what he could to ensure that Jenna and I got the best care possible. Dr. Eastman was in contact with the best doctors possible in Seattle, and throughout the entire ordeal, he remained an advocate we could call in case we had questions or concerns.

Scripps Health came through in many other ways, too. I was told that Chris Van Gorder (whom I had had the opportunity to get to know in Leadership Academy and so admired for his leadership), Dr. Eastman (who I already thought as a role model and hero) and June Komar (a corporate vice president, someone I know well and think of as the best, smartest and nicest executive in the company) would be flying to visit me in a few days. That was a single point of focus that helped me get through that rough first week.

When the Scripps leadership team came, they brought along one of my managers, Kenneth Campbell. Together my colleagues reviewed my plan of care and made sure Marilyn was OK. That was an enormous relief.

Chris also told me that I did not need to worry, and that the entire Scripps organization was behind me. Based on all the well wishes and cards that kept coming in, I knew that was 100 percent true. I apologized to Chris that I could not come back to work after vacation as I had initially planned, but that I would probably figure out a way to return as soon as possible, and that I could work with a halo. (I had no idea what I was talking about, but Chris is such a motivating person that he makes you feel you can do nearly anything as long as you believe in it. He's a very good enabler for the *stubborn*.)

With my good eye, and in my mind, I can still see Chris and June bending forward over my bed, comforting me, and behind them the entire Scripps organization. They gave me yet another goal to look forward to: They told me Gary Fybel, the chief executive of the hospital I worked in, and my boss, Mary Jo Webb, would come the next week. I had to do well, stay alive, and be ready for their visit.

That first week I spent at Harbor View Medical Center in Seattle was the most difficult week of my life. After the seven-hour surgery just to "clean me up" and the ten-hour surgery to fix my scalp, my severed wrist tendon, eyelid, and whatever else needed to be fixed, I also had to endure getting a halo put on my head.

Getting My Halo

The halo device, designed in the 1950s, is still one of the most effective devices used to immobilize a broken spine so that the bones can heal. It's basically a large circular metal ring, about twice the circumference of the skull, which rests on your shoulders and immobilizes your head through the use of screws.

When I was told in the ICU that it was time for my halo to be put on, I was actually looking forward to it. In case it hasn't already come through, I'm a bit *stubborn*. The fact that the medical staff had listened to my request for a halo made me feel as if I was at least a little bit in charge of my own care.

I was wheeled into an area with a lot of white curtains, bright lights, and three people. They all seemed to be going about their business, which was putting a halo on a patient. I do not remember them paying too much attention to me. That was OK, because I prefer people to be serious about their work rather than being too nice and forgetting crucial things.

Unfortunately, this time they were a bit too concentrated on the technical aspect of their work, and I became just a little bit too irrelevant.

The explanation of the halo was routine; I was already familiar with the device as they explained what was going to happen. What they did not explain was how I was going to feel and what I was going to feel.

The device was positioned around my head and pressure was applied on all sides. They started tightening something, and it hurt. It hurt a lot—and that was *weird*, especially for a person who was quite drugged at the time.

I yelled out that it hurt. The two men in regular street clothes, who I assumed were the equipment people, looked up at the physician. The doctor said, "I think we forgot to give him lidocaine."

I could agree with that, because there was a lot of superficial pain—they had been about to screw something directly into my head without local anesthesia.

Lidocaine injections were given, and the team suddenly paid a lot more attention to me.

After about twenty minutes, to give the injections time to numb my skin, the process continued. Screws were drilled straight into my skull. This process was extremely painful. I could hear bones crack and I felt that if they screwed it any tighter my skull would crack open like a walnut. The local pain killer had certainly numbed the skin, but this was such a deep kind of pain that only being put completely out could have stopped me from feeling it. Marilyn later commented that it reminded her of medieval torture.

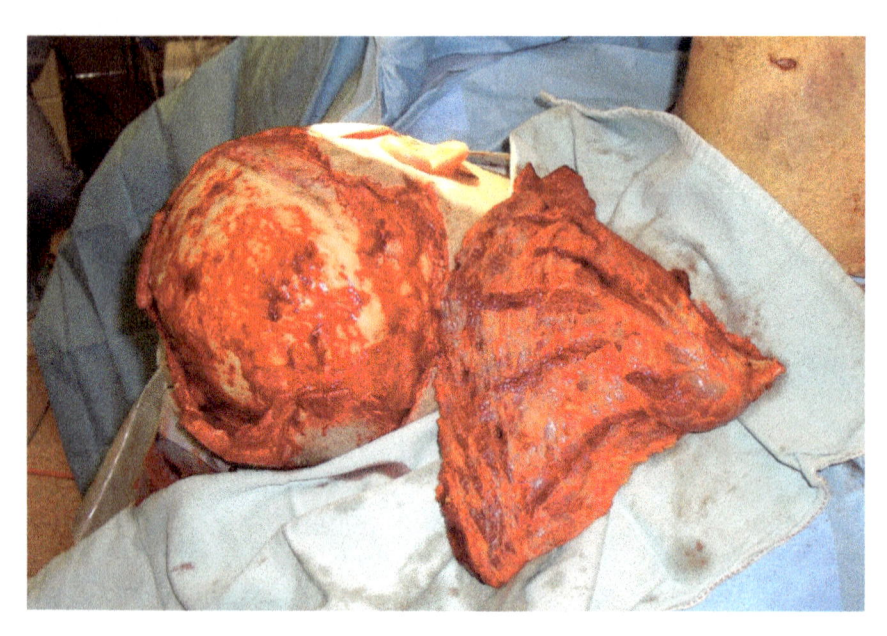

CHAPTER 7

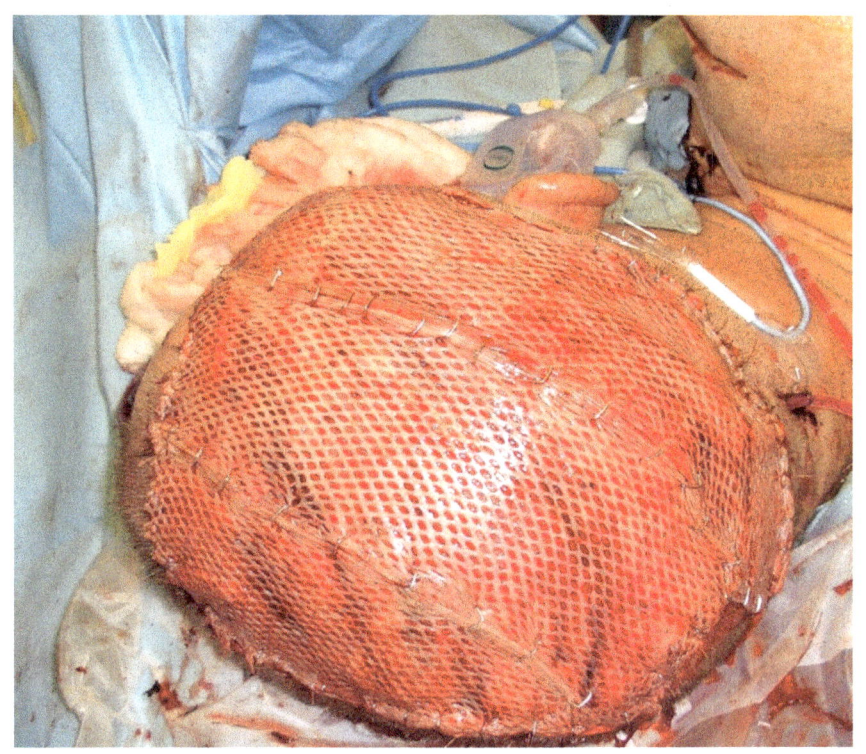

My head during and after surgery. The beautiful "steak" is my lattisimus dorsi—a muscle from my back. The "netting" on my head is skin from my right thigh.

Back in the hospital unit, wound care had also started. I had claw and bite wounds on every extremity, which meant at least ninety minutes of dressing changes daily. I actually enjoyed these sessions; it felt good to get cleaned, and I liked the attention.

The halo, however, was horrible.

I remember waking up one time feeling completely tied down and claustrophobic, unable to move my head or back, unable to turn, and as if I was pinned down onto my hospital bed. Regardless of my comfort (or lack thereof), I could not move.

I panicked, but luckily, Marilyn helped me to calm down. She and the RN decided I needed to be on some anti-panic medication, which ended up helping me tremendously. I was also still on morphine for pain, because by now pain had become a major issue. During the bear attack and rescue operation itself I had minimal pain, but once in the hospital, pain became a huge burden. Self-administration of pain meds did not work well for me, because I would not remember to push the button until I was in bad pain, or the button would be lost in the bed and I could not find it with my hand. At one time I remember waking up in the middle of the night, screaming for help since the RN bell and all else seemed to be out of reach, and I had a major panic attack. It seemed assistance would never arrive. Finally, after forty-five minutes, an injection and the RN's presence calmed me down again.

While I was in the surgical intensive care unit (SICU), seconds seemed like minutes and minutes like hours. I would sleep and wake up thinking it was the next day only to find out it was still the same hour when I had fallen asleep. Marilyn held constant vigil and kept me sane. Her strength and patience are incredible. I never saw her cry and she was always upbeat, telling me I would be fine.

At one point I asked one of the residents if I would die because I did not know if I could handle the pain and inactivity any more. He said, "No way. You will live and you are already over the hump." Marilyn was there to totally support that conclusion and talk some sense into me.

Finally, after a full week, I was transferred out of SICU to another floor, and into a private room. Being transported from bed to bed, or to radiology or surgery, was always an adventure—one I did not enjoy. It was the scariest thing to lie on my back and be helpless. I also became extremely aware of all the bumps in the hallways, especially with the halo; that seemed to increase the vibration into my bones. I also always wondered if the transport guys really knew all the things wrong with me, so during every trip down the hallway on a gurney, I would keep reminding them, "No pressure at the back of the head because my skin graft can't take that. Please be careful since I broke C2. All four of my extremities have wounds so don't hold onto anything very tight."

In time, I would become much more mobile and insist on walking to the transport gurney, or even crawling onto the surgery table.

Despite my concern, all the transporters were great, and never did hurt me, but what an appreciation I acquired for patients who are moved all the time.

My new room was comfortable and I felt much more relaxed. It was quiet and had a window. The first few nights in that room I was still kind of silly from the medications. I had hallucinations that my room was a connecting passage between a gym and locker room and folks had to walk through my room to get dressed or cleaned up all the time. I distinctly remember that the locker room was on the right side, and I did not mind that people had to use my room to walk through. There was also a huge black sculpture in the middle of the room that everyone had to walk around. It was made of artificial material in the shape of the Batmobile, yet it had faces sculpted into it. Again, no one seemed to mind that they had to walk around this in order to take care of me.

I remember later telling Marilyn about these perceptions and that I did know they were hallucinations; it was just really interesting. Thank God they only lasted until I became mobile enough to walk around and see for myself that there was no locker room or sculpture in my room.

Oh, how I wanted to get up, and a few days after I transferred to the regular med-surgical floor it was finally that time.

Before I get into that experience, I have to preface the situation.

The halo informational brochure showed a picture of this guy walking with a halo at the airport as if it was no big deal; naturally, I thought it would be a breeze. Well, it was a big deal. It felt as if my neck muscles were not strong enough to keep this metal "head cage" up, and I had to feel with my left hand to reassure myself that I did indeed have muscles back there and that they were working and holding up my head and halo just fine. After that initial shock, getting up was great.

The first time I tried walking, I went nearly one hundred feet, and I doubled my distance every day after that. The physical therapist and occupational therapist walked me to the windows to see outside with my one good eye, and I saw an antenna. "Is that the famous Seattle landmark?" I asked. They all laughed, because it was just an antenna, not the Space Needle. But hey, I was able to look outside. What a treat.

Meanwhile, Back on the Trail with Jenna…

In the meantime, Jenna had been released from Kalispell and was able to join me for a few days. My wife's cousin Kim had some flight miles saved up and was able to donate those to Jenna to get her to Seattle.

What a wonderful sight to see her and how great she looked!

One of the first things she said to me was, "Dad, I guess I need to thank you for saving my life." That touched me deeply. Although I was only following my instinct, that was what I had wanted—for the bear not to hurt Jenna and to take me instead.

Like me, Jenna was conscious during most of the attack, although she thinks she may have passed out before her fall. Jenna recalls that when we went around a dead corner in the trail, the bear and her two cubs were maybe five feet in front of her. I was still trotting forward but Jenna stopped, took two steps back to me, and the bear was upon us. She says she tried to get to the bear spray, which we had attached in what we thought was a handy spot on our backpack, but of course we had no idea we would actually need to use it. And anyway, the impact of the bear had knocked the spray onto the trail.

Jenna remembered picking it up and trying to use it while the bear charged her. At the time she thought it was not working, but in retrospect, we think she didn't exactly pull the white safety switch off (because when you're panicking, who thinks to do that?). We also thought, incorrectly, that it was probably a good thing, because the bear could have become so enraged at being sprayed, it would have attacked her instead of going after me. Actually, if a bear is sprayed, even in close proximity, it is unlikely to attack, but instead will retreat.

After her failure to discharge the bear spray, Jenna thinks she may have passed out very briefly but awakened moments later to realize that she was in mid-fall and had her eyes closed. She landed hard on a ledge about thirty-to-fifty feet under the trail, but was able to stand up and scramble under a bush and assume the fetal position. She remembers seeing the bear on top of me, but not seeing me, just hearing me scream. I do not recall screaming, but I am sure I did. For Jenna, this was the worst sound she'd ever heard.

After I had rolled over this ledge for the last time, the bear ambled over to Jenna, who was lying in a fetal position. She saw it coming and instinctively grabbed the bear by the head to keep it away. This was probably not the best thing to do since this gave the bear full frontal access to her face. The bear bit her once, tearing open the right corner of her mouth and leaving two incisor puncture wounds on top of her head.

Jenna did not move.

The bear then grabbed and bit her right shoulder. Again, Jenna did not move and played dead.

Because of her extreme calm and strength not to move, the bear must have thought that she had now taken care of both of us; we were either dead or at least no threat anymore. And so she walked away.

Jenna also did not know if I was still alive or dead—until she heard my voice calling to her several minutes later.

— CHAPTER 8 —
The Road to Recovery: Seattle

It was now thirteen days into my hospitalization. The hallucinations were gone, I was sleeping well, and I was trying to stay as mobile as I could.

I remember doing some arm and leg movements while watching music videos on TV. Grunge didn't work, but rap, R&B, and pop songs were good enough for me to get some exercise.

The thirteenth day also held another much-anticipated visit: my boss, Mary Jo (MJ), and our hospital's chief executive, Gary. Much to their surprise, I met them in the hallway on my way back from a physical therapy session. These two administrators brought their well wishes as well as messages and cards from the entire hospital staff. They presented me with a ten-foot-long get-well card from the employees of the hospital system (along with many single get-well cards and even some monetary gifts). That brought me to tears. I felt such warmth and love coming from all of the people I worked with, and I didn't feel I deserved it.

In fact, I did not realize that changeable emotions were to become a part of my future life. My ability to talk about the attack was hampered by my emotions. Anytime I would get to a part about people who helped us, I would just start sobbing. The harder I tried to suppress the tears, the more difficult it would become to talk about any part of the attack and rescue. Talking about the hikers who helped us on the trail made me cry, the generosity shown by all my co-workers made me cry, and on and on. It started to become annoying.

In the Seattle hospital room, Gary shared some wisdom with me; he said that when people die or are critically injured, only then do we really know how they've lived their lives. He had learned this when his father had passed away. Gary told me the outpouring of love from my coworkers came because I must have made a difference in their lives.

If I were a different person—a bully or a cold tyrant who did not treat people with respect—then this outpouring may not have happened.

Later in the visit, Gary shared another piece of information with me: my skull had the marks of the bear on it.

Up to that point, no one had confirmed with me what I had expected—that one of the bear's teeth actually did go into my skull. I verified this information with the physician who was taking the bandage off my graft. He paused when I asked and he had to swallow a bit before he could answer since the question caught him by surprise. "Yes, you had tooth and claw marks on the skull," he answered. This information was significant to me because it confirmed again that I hadn't imagined what I had gone through.

Gary and Mary Jo stayed for at least four hours. MJ, a former nurse, even emptied my catheter bag and Gary held my hand many times to convey his best wishes. I already knew that I worked for a great organization; they just proved it again and again.

During the visit, Marilyn and I learned that our insurance had approved my transportation back home by ambulance plane and that this would happen on Friday—the 15th day after the attack. I was going home!

This surprised my RN, who didn't think I was ready to go home yet, but I explained to her that I would be going to Scripps Memorial Hospital, La Jolla, my work home or home away from home, and that I was looking forward to being with all my coworkers again.

After Gary and MJ left, I had renewed energy.

The day before their visit I had been in a funk. There had been a misunderstanding with the surgery department's scheduling. The surgery to fix my eye socket fracture had been scheduled, and I had been prepared with NPO status (i.e., no food or drink by mouth; this is to prevent any aspiration during anesthesia).

The following morning, Marilyn and I became concerned when 9:00 a.m. rolled around and no one had yet come to get me for surgery. Apparently, everyone working on my case knew about the scheduled surgery except for the surgeon who was scheduled to perform it!

After a lot of work from a discharge planner, Heidi, and the great good will of the surgeon, we did get to reschedule surgery a little late, at 5:30 p.m. Even then, my surgery was held up by another trauma in the operating room. But by 6:30 p.m., I was rolled in.

My surgeon had told Marilyn and me that in addition to a fractured eye socket, I also had a severed muscle and that there was less than a 50 percent chance that he could fix it, but he would try. At least the fracture would be fixed. He also stated up front that he would not be able to stay for the entire procedure.

In the end, he did stay for the entire three hour procedure, and indeed, they could not find the severed muscle. He said that another surgeon could possibly find it. A CT scan the next day confirmed there was a muscle left. Now I needed to find a doctor who could reconnect it.

That is where Dr. Eastman came back into the picture. One of the MDs he had organized to take over my care at Scripps was an excellent ophthalmologist.

My final two days at Harbor View were filled with more progress, great nursing care and preparations for going home.

I also had a press conference scheduled! This was the first time that I became aware our story held great interest for the media. The press conference was actually great fun, and occurred only one hour before I was wheeled out of the hospital to go to the hospital plane. Marilyn was also present and was asked some questions herself, which I think she answered in great style. Of course, most of the attention was on me, but the real stars were the physicians who had performed my surgeries, the emergency care team, and the plastic surgeons—especially Dr. Nicholas Vedder, who had reconstructed my scalp. At the conference he explained how he had taken the latissimus dorsi (a shoulder/back muscle) from my back and had grafted that muscle onto my bare-bone skull. He then covered the muscle with skin from my right thigh. Everyone was incredibly impressed by the outcome—he gave me my head back again.

After the doctors were interviewed, the transport folks wheeled me in. We were on the news and had our picture taken. Everyone seemed amazed about our positive attitude, but what else could we do? I could have been dead many times over. Jenna could have been dead or hurt much worse. Neither of those outcomes happened. I could only be happy and grateful for all the excellent care that I had received, and that Jenna was already home. So I shared with the reporters something that Gary, my chief administrator, had said to me during his visit that had also helped my outlook: "There are many people who spend the rest of their lives asking 'Why me?' when dealing with injuries like yours, Johan. Well, you know your answer to 'why me.' It was you because it wasn't Jenna!"

In my world, that made perfect sense. My entire goal during the struggle with the grizzly was to protect Jenna, and I had won. Although I had some difficult times as I healed, I just had to look at Jenna to feel much better again.

One reporter asked Marilyn if I was always like this (upbeat), and she responded, "Oh yes."

After the news conference, we were returned to the hospital room, where we waited for our transport plane. I was going to miss the awesome people in Seattle. They put me back together again and gave me lots of hope for a nearly full recovery.

At this point in my hospitalization, I was now able to go to the regular bathroom and wash my hands at a regular sink. A regular sink meant there was a mirror above it.

Shall I look?

Oh well, why not?

Holy crap, I look horrible!

But hey, I can still see myself, and it isn't that bad.

One more obstacle out of the way. I now knew I looked pretty beat up.

My ability to talk about the attack was hampered by my emotions. Anytime I would get to a part about people who helped us, I would just start sobbing. The harder I tried to suppress the tears, the more difficult it would become to talk about any part of the attack and rescue.

Talking about the hikers who helped us on the trail made me cry, the generosity shown by all my co-workers made me cry, and on and on. It started to become annoying.

When I got wheeled out of the hospital, I had my first breath of fresh air and even a few drops of Seattle rain. That was all I got to see of Seattle, but I knew I would return to visit everyone after I healed.

Once we arrived at the small, municipal airport, we got a look at the plane we would be flying in. Marilyn nearly had a heart attack when she saw the small size of it, but she told me her little panic was nothing compared to the ordeal I had been through, so she would just deal with it.

The "hospital bed" in this plane was so narrow that I could not fit the width of my whole body on it, and I am fairly skinny. I asked if I could instead sit reclined in the seats that they had, which ended up working much better. I was comfortable enough for the three-and-a-half hour trip home, and Marilyn kept me entertained with her scared faces and body jerks when unexpected sounds came from the cockpit, or during turbulence.

All kidding aside, the woman to whom I am married, who claims she is afraid of flying, stayed very calm and relaxed. The medic and pilot were great and continuously made sure that we were comfortable.

Of course, I did have to tell my attack story again…but that was fine.

— CHAPTER 9 —
The Road to Recovery: San Diego

When we landed in overcast San Diego, an ambulance was waiting to bring me home to Scripps Memorial Hospital, La Jolla.

It was incredibly bizarre to return to Scripps by ambulance and to be wheeled down the hall and up to the 4th floor as a patient. Both daughters were in the room waiting for me, and I noticed that Scripps had arranged for me to be in their best corner room.

The transfer from ambulance stretcher to hospital bed was kind of rough. The plane's medic had come along to ensure everything went well, but he was taken aback by the transport team's less-then-satisfactory technique. Unfortunately my head started bleeding since the graft tore open a bit. Apparently a lot of the fluid from the graft had accumulated at the occiput (the back of the head, where the skull joins the spine), so any small wound resulted in an immediate trickle of blood. Once we changed the bed and were settled in I was ridiculously happy.

Right away, some of my coworkers came up to visit me, and that stream of visitors did not let up for the next two weeks. I felt so loved. Some people purposely stayed away because they wanted me to get some rest, but either way, I appreciated both the rest time I was given and the visits I received.

My experience at Scripps was different than Harbor View because now my medical condition was less acute and less painful. Yet lots of work still had to be done. First up was my eye.

Now that I had some vision in the right eye, I was no longer satisfied with just that; I wanted it all back, if possible, and along came Dr. Arthur Perry.

Dr. Eastman had recommended him, and when he visited me he gave me no false hope. He said if I were one of his own family members, he would advise me to have surgery ASAP to see if the muscle could be found and reattached. The longer we waited, the more chance of muscle atrophy. He also said that if the nerve to the muscle had been cut, repairing the muscle would not matter; it would be non-functional anyway. In that sense, it was to be a kind of exploratory surgery. This conversation was on a Saturday; when he suggested doing the surgery soon, he meant, "What about 7:30 a.m. tomorrow?"

That worked for me.

I was in great spirits on Sunday morning. The surgeon had explained to me that I would be awake for the procedure because he would have to ask me to move my eyes. That turned out to be much less scary than it sounded. I was sedated enough that I had no pain, but more importantly, it also did not bother me that someone was poking and stitching in my eye. What I feared more was that he would look at the muscle and say something like, "No, this does not look good," or "What a mess!" I'm thankful none of that happened.

There was a lot of digging; at one point he said, "I feel the muscle, I just do not see it." That made me extremely happy, because that meant that the muscle was moving, so the nerve was still intact. And indeed, moments later he located bits and pieces of the muscle and started sewing things together. He also located another muscle that a hospital report had stated was damaged, but I remember him calling the surgical nurse over and saying, "Look what excellent condition this one is in."

I was asked to look down frequently and although my eye was doing that, I never had that sensation so I continually asked the RN, "Is my eye moving down?" She replied with a very strong "Yes!" That was reassuring.

I asked Dr. Perry if this surgery was going better than expected and he replied in the affirmative. How happy I was!

When they got me back to the room, I gave a thumbs-up to my waiting family who all were very excited; this meant that with time, my eyes would recover nearly all their original function. I still had to expect double vision and would have to train my eyes and brain to see normally again, a process that could take up to six months. There might even have to be some fine-tuning surgeries to get both eyes to work together again perfectly, but I was grateful.

The next day was slated to be spine day. A total of three hours of radiological studies had been scheduled to happen after my three-hour eye surgery, but my dear RN, Sarah, told radiology that this could not happen after the eye surgery because I needed my rest first before going through the radiology mill.

So on Monday morning at 8:00 a.m., I was in radiology. I knew I would have three tests: a CT scan, an MRI and an X-ray. I was concerned about the MRI because of the metal halo around my head; you are trained in hospitals to keep metal out of MRI rooms, as the machine itself is a giant magnet, and metals around MRIs can be deadly hazards. But I was assured that it was not an issue.

I was still worried.

The CT scan was a piece of cake; just an uncomfortable small table, but it was over in minutes. I expected the same from the MRI, but boy was I wrong. I did not know this would be a 45-minute test and that it would hurt. I initially became restless and had them pull me out of the tube because the sound really hurt above my ear, and I had visions of a metal staple used to hold my skull graft down that they must have forgotten I had being pulled straight out by the magnet. But I was assured there was nothing there and that an MRI could be uncomfortable.

Uncomfortable it was! Every time the MRI made a sound, the pins in my skull would hurt like someone gently pushing a sharp knife into my skin. I also made the mistake of opening my left eye while in "the tube" and if I was not claustrophobic yet, I certainly was claustrophobic then. I wanted to get the test over with as soon as possible, so I relaxed as much as I could and thought all kinds of good thoughts about my birds.

As it turned out, I survived the radiology experience, although I do not think anyone will ever get me into an MRI again without heavy sedation. During those forty-five minutes of pain, I think I used up all my calming stories.

The X-ray experience after the MRI was not nearly as bad. It was just difficult for the radiology technicians to position me because of my halo. When I got back to the room, I was wiped out and grateful that Sarah had been able to postpone this experience, because indeed, if this had happened the day after a three-hour surgery, I think I would have passed out.

Although my eyes and neck were taken care of for the moment, my wounds were still a major issue.

Marilyn and the RNs had counted twenty-one punctures or tears, including my scalp. Some gashes were very deep, some isolated, and others clustered together. I felt I was in great hands with my wound care nurse, Lorena, and the physical therapy (PT) department. It was kind of different to be taken care of by my own staff, but I knew how good they were and I trusted them completely. In fact, I was very impressed with the entire collaboration between PT, occupational therapy (OT), wound care, and nursing. Collectively, they all worked to do what was best for me.

The MD overseeing my care plan was the head of plastics, Dr. Scott Bartlebort. I had daily interactions with him. His bedside manner was excellent. He would always shake my hand (by the way, he had the softest hands, we all noticed) and make eye contact when he spoke. I knew he was very patient/person-oriented. He decided that all my bite wounds (which were still open for healing purposes) could now be closed, which would eliminate 90 percent of all wound care, and then I could get ready for discharge. Friday would be the day this would happen—three weeks and one day after the attack.

Upon awakening on Friday, I was excited to be one step closer to being healed.

Right before surgery I reminded everyone that the graft on my skull could not tolerate direct pressure so they would make sure that I was positioned correctly. Now that I was this far along, I would have really hated for anything to hamper my recovery.

The surgery release form had stated that the doctor might need to use a graft, so my first concern in the recovery room was if they indeed had used one. Luckily, they had not. However, the surgery did end up taking twice as long as expected, and around 4 p.m. I returned to my room. This had turned into a six-plus hour job instead of three hours, and my body sure felt it. It took me a good two days to get my energy level back to where it was before surgery.

One great benefit was that the surgeon had been able to remove the scabby skin that was on my thigh graft, so that eliminated a lot of itching and pain, and now nearly all my wounds were closed. Two wounds on my left hamstring proved to be too deep and would require some continuing wound care, but everything else was closed.

All went well until Saturday night.

I woke up needing to go to the bathroom. While there, I started to shiver and feel very cold, as if I had a fever. The RN tucked the blankets around me in bed and gave me heated blankets to keep me warm. The next morning I awoke hot and sweaty. My vitals showed that I had a fever of 101. At the same time, my right arm was swollen, red, and itchy, indicating an infection.

I now had to be placed on contact isolation precautions. This meant that all visitors and health care personnel had to wear a protective layer between their clothing and me. In my case, that meant everyone had to wear an extra gown and gloves. This places a barrier between the patient and the caregiver. It was not easy for anyone to just come in the room and check in on me because it would mean a few minutes had to be spent putting the isolation garb on.

Dr. Bartlebort had to go back in and open most of my arm again to clean out pus and other infectious fluids. It was rather unbelievable that within twenty-four hours after surgery, Marilyn and the PT staff were already pushing lots of infectious material out of my arm.

It got worse: the infection turned out to be MRSA (methicillin-resistant staphococcus aurelius), which is no laughing matter, because as a drug-resistant infection, it's very difficult to treat. Dr. Chang, the hospital's infection-control MD, became part of my care team. She is known for being extremely meticulous, and she spent hours with me. She ordered tests to make sure that the infection was not in the bone and put me on a very heavy antibiotic that had to go in via IV. Unfortunately, the veins in my left arm, which are regular IV sites, were hard to find, and once they were established, the medication would occasionally get backed up and create painful hard spots in my arm.

By Wednesday I was definitively diagnosed, and wound care and medication was on track. PT and wound care staff decided that a vacuum cleansing system (called a V.A.C.) would be best for me, so I ended up with one at my hamstring and one at my right arm. The V.A.C. creates a negative pressure at the wound and continuously sucks on it to take pus and drainage away from the wound. It also helps the wound to heal faster.

Once the V.A.C. was established and the IV meds were decided on, there was no need for me to be in a hospital anymore.

I could go home. Really *home*.

A few more things had to happen first. Since the IV antibiotics were so aggressive, a PICC line (peripherally inserted central catheter) had to be established. This type of IV goes in a vein in your upper arm and the line ends in your heart. The person who inserted the line was a Physician Assistant named Shawn, and I remembered hiring him into the Scripps system as a PT. It was sure great to be able to benefit from great folks that I had the good fortune to know. The peripheral IV line that I had before the PICC line was painful and left my arm sore where the antibiotics had gone in. After this PICC line, though, I had no discomfort.

— CHAPTER 10 —
Discharge: Going Home

The day of my discharge was finally here.

After four weeks and one day, it was time to go home. My brother, Gerard, and his wife, Tineke, had come from the Netherlands a few days earlier to assist Marilyn for my return home. We Dutch tend to be very stoic people, so there normally isn't a lot of extra emotional turmoil going on around us. That relaxes everyone around them. In Holland, we say, "Just act normal, because that is crazy enough."

Knowing my brother and sister-in-law were here helped me to focus on the short-term goals I needed to achieve in the hospital, so that I could go home and forget about what might happen a year from now. Their visit also brought out the practical Dutch in me. *Why worry about the things that you can't control and that may or may not happen? Focus on those things that you do control, like your attitude, and be helpful to all the health care workers who want to assist you.*

The hospital had told us the date and time I would be discharged to go home, and I was certainly looking forward to it. On D-Day (discharge day) morning, I asked my nurse what else would be happening before I could go home, and she seemed a bit flustered, as if she didn't entirely know what was going on. She informed me that the discharge orders were not fully completed yet.

"Well, that should be easy to do," I said, "Just call the doctors."

Oh, how wrong I was.

The nurses had trouble getting hold of some of the doctors, but I was determined to go home that day.

Stubborn.

In the end, a trauma doctor who had never treated me had to come in to write my discharge medication orders. He was a bit nervous about that, but I assured him that the medications he was writing prescriptions for were the meds that I had been taking, and that I needed them to be able to tolerate the halo.

Like clockwork, Gerard and Marilyn appeared in my room at 10:00 am to take me home, but there were still no signs of an actual discharge yet. I was just lying in bed, fully dressed, but no one seemed to know when I could leave.

The RN in charge had written some discharge instructions on a piece of paper for me, but she had not given me a copy yet. I had the prescriptions for my medication and all we needed now was a way to get the wound-cleansing V.A.C. home with me. It was literally the one thing preventing me from leaving. (We later found out that no one had arranged for the V.A.C. to be used at home.)

I was becoming increasingly agitated.

By noon, two hours past my anticipated discharge time, I had had it.

I studied the small and probably portable V.A.C. attached to my arm and asked the physical therapist who happened to be treating me, "Does this thing work on battery power?" He said, "It certainly does." I don't think he expected my next move, which was to unplug the unit, get up and tell my family, "Let's go!"

We all walked to the front desk secretary at the nurses' station, some of us slightly embarrassed, but I couldn't help it.

I was *out of there.*

The secretary looked up at me and said, "Can I help you?" Behind her, my RN was trying to make the copy of the handwritten medication discharge instructions she'd written out for me earlier.

"Yes. I have been a patient here for two weeks, and I was supposed to be discharged at 10:00 a.m., and I want to go home, but I still need my copy of the instructions the RN behind you has written for me."

The RN apologized, made a quick copy of her note and handed me her original. Then I set off for the elevators, with family in tow, along with some of the PT staff that were both coworkers and my treating therapists.

Gerard went ahead to ready the "getaway car."

In retrospect, I realize I was obnoxious. But it was that important to me to get back home. Part of the reason why I was so anxious to leave was that my brother and his wife would be leaving to go back home to the Netherlands later that afternoon, and I wanted to spend just a little bit of time with them at my home before they left for the airport.

When I arrived home, I saw that the hospital bed we had ordered at been set up downstairs in the TV room of our two story house, where all the bedrooms where upstairs.

Way back in Seattle, Marilyn had figured that to have me be comfortable lying on my back and to avoid any pressure on my graft, a hospital bed would be needed. She would roll up two small towels and put them under each rod at the back of my halo, which was much easier to do if I was in an adjustable bed. That was great advice—although sleeping on my back was still tough. But medication works wonders, and the pain and anti-anxiety pills helped a lot, as did a nightly sleeping pill.

Coming home after a full month of traumatic events like these was strange and somehow anticlimactic—but in a very good way.

But other issues arose.

As a result of having contracted MRSA in the hospital, I still had to be on an IV drip of strong antibiotics twice a day. This medication had to be delivered through the PICC line that deposited it straight into my heart.

A day or two before my discharge, the nursing staff in the hospital had explained and demonstrated PICC medication administration to me in an understandable way, but there was an issue. They had demonstrated a rather simple-looking, easy enough process to me—the doped-up patient who had probably suffered at least minor head trauma during the bear attack—but they had *not* demonstrated this to Marilyn, who would be administering my IV medication.

When Marilyn found out she would be doing this, she freaked.

She was livid that no one had explained and demonstrated the process to her. The nursing staff did not have time to go through the whole demonstration again—not because they did not want to, but because it could only be done when medication needed to be administered. (A nurse did come and verbally went over the steps with Marilyn, but that isn't the same thing).

Now it was the first time Marilyn was going to administer my meds at home. But without having actually practiced, Marilyn did not know how to flush the IV line. We kind of started it together, but there was an air bubble in the line. Of course Marilyn worried she would give me an embolism, and secretly I wondered, "Oh my God, can that kill me?" As we despaired, wondering what to do, I happened to glance at my arm. I saw that the V.A.C. had started to bubble as well, and it seemed the seal had been broken.

We were a sorry sight.

Luckily, we have cultivated many friendships through the years with people in the health care field. Marilyn called a friend who is an RN. She came over right away and was sublime in educating us on the simple process of flushing the IV line. And she informed us that an air bubble would not kill me.

Whew.

With that problem taken care of, we still had to figure out the V.A.C. issue. To the rescue came my PT manager at La Jolla, who also lives in Escondido. She came over, redressed my wound, and reapplied the V.A.C. to create a new seal.

Now, maybe she should have left well enough alone, but Marilyn was still appalled that we had not had adequate home instruction for troubleshooting issues that could come up. She insisted that I call the discharge planners at the hospital and explain what had happened as a result of incomplete discharge planning. She figured that since I worked at Scripps in patient care, it would be beneficial for the discharge team to know, so they could help other patients avoid unnecessary stress.

I called the next day and spoke to my case manager. I tried to be nice.

Right away, I got pushback.

Marilyn heard me and mouthed, "You are too nice. What happened to us should never happen to anyone." And then she took the phone from me.

What ensued after that was *not* a good discussion, and it went from bad to worse. The nurse case manager kept telling us that we had been instructed in home care, and she was half right. But Marilyn had never received full instructions, and she kept insisting that they should take some responsibility for their insufficient process. The phone came back to me. I can still hear the manager ask, "So Johan, what do you want us to do about this?"

Well. I didn't know because the problems had been solved, but I offered that they should never discharge a patient this way again without making sure the primary caregiver fully understood his or her responsibilities.

The next day, a home health RN came. Unfortunately, she was struggling because she did not have adequate notes from the hospital telling her what services to give me. Marilyn and I explained, but she was perplexed that the information she had was so poor.

It got worse.

While the home health RN was working on me, we received a phone call. It was one of the trauma doctors; actually, the chair of the trauma department.

Instead of asking about the reasons we'd called the previous day or offering an apology, he lashed out at Marilyn for daring to complain. "Johan was treated like a king," he blared at her, and so on. Marilyn was confounded at the barrage, and for only the second time during this entire episode, she cried.

I was not proud of my hospital at that point.

I called my boss later and explained. She understood and would follow up.

Ugh.

(I was later placed in charge of patient satisfaction for our hospital and was able to use this experience to make significant positive changes.)

The home health RN came every other day to keep track of numerous wounds and monitor how my body was holding up with the heavy antibiotics. The care was superb, and I wish I could remember the name of the RN who took care of me.

Things started to settle into a routine. Twice a day I had to sit for ninety minutes with a Vencomycin drip in my arm. The V.A.C. was sucking along and occasionally throwing a fit. We had many friends come over to offer their well wishes. The mothers from the dance team that Stephanie and Jenna belonged to brought dinners for us for the next three months.

A Car for Stephanie

I had befriended several PT patients over the years, and one couple was the Warners. They are great people, very down to earth, and had moved away from the San Diego area, but Tom, the husband, had heard about what happened to me.

I was excited to hear from him, and he immediately asked what he could do for me. I couldn't think of a thing, but he was persistent. Anything he could do for the girls, Marilyn, or me. Then I remembered—Tom had always been into cars. So when he asked me again what he could do for me, I asked if he could help us find a nice, safe, used car for Stephanie.

In all this commotion around Jenna and me, we had kind of lost Stephanie. Not that she was complaining or anything, because that is not who she is, but we have two daughters—not one.

Stephanie had turned sixteen. We needed to get her some wheels. But I was in no condition to find them for her. Tom told me he would take care of it. A couple weeks later, Tom called. Being a fastidious and to-the-point guy, he asked, "Does she like blue?" It took me a moment to figure out what he was talking about, but then

I put it together.

I yelled out to Stephanie, "Steph, do you like blue?"

"For what?" she asked.

"A car."

"Sure," she answered.

I repeated this brief conversation to Tom, who said, "Good. We are on our way." Within fifteen minutes he was driving up the driveway in a brand new Hyundai, with the salesman in tow. Stephanie was so surprised she didn't know what to say.

Meanwhile, Tom was acting like a car salesman, telling us about all the virtues of this car and what a great deal it was for Stephanie! We really didn't need to be convinced. That day Stephanie became the owner of a brand new car. Tom hadn't just totally come through; he came through beyond our imagination.

That is what real friends do. You don't keep a list of "I do this for you, and now you do this for me."

You do what your friends need.

Friends from Holland

After my brother had returned home, I got a call from my best friend in Holland, Rita. That was a great call—she would be my next visitor from Holland. Rita and I had become great friends from our first day in PT school in Amsterdam. We were both young (seventeen and eighteen) and from The Polder. We both had parents who came from a farming background. Because of our similarities, Rita was like a sister to me, and we went through some great student experiences together.

I also met Greetje, Rita's older sister, during that time. She had already lived in Amsterdam for a while, so she knew the ropes, and Rita and I looked to Greetje as the wise and calm one. More than once we found our way to her house to vent our frustrations about the amount of studying we had to do.

Rita, her longtime partner Henk, and Greetje arrived from Holland soon after Stephanie got her car. I looked at their visit as a mini-vacation; they had come over thinking they would have to take care of me. To their great surprise, I wasn't lying around moaning in bed, but instead greeted them at the door.

For the next week, their visit became a welcome distraction. I went for my first meal outside the house with them—of course, that had to be at an In 'n' Out because that was the best hamburger fast food place in town at the time. We also went to the San Diego Zoo together. Mind you, I was still wearing my halo, and it was quite an experience getting in and out of the car without dinging the brace or the car. On the other hand, walking the Zoo's expansive grounds and steep hills was fine. I just couldn't move as fast as my normal pace.

Navigating the Zoo was another milestone for my recovery. I remember all of the little things that happened that day—stuff I normally would take for granted. Two things, especially, stood out. The first was standing in front of the lowland gorilla viewing area. There was quite a crowd gathered at the incredibly thick, reinforced window because the animals were all very close to the glass, including the big silverback male. I could only imagine how strong he was and what damage he could do if he wanted to.

A young woman and her husband were there at the same time, looking at the animals, and when she saw me standing there with my halo on, she asked what had happened to me.

"Did you have a car accident?"

"No, I was attacked by a grizzly bear."

I was very matter of fact about it, which she must have read as deadpan humor. She burst out laughing and said, "Yeah, right." I didn't have the heart to correct her, since she thought that was just so funny. I let it be.

The other standout experience came a few minutes later, when we passed the grizzly bear enclosure. My friends asked me if I was comfortable with seeing that, and I said, "Sure, why not." As we viewed the bears, one of them was gnawing on a large bone with white cartilage exposed. It was weird to see; this bear was chewing on a bone just as a bear had chewed on my bare skull only two months before.

I decided that it was good for me to have seen this, though, because it meant that I could handle exposure to a potentially upsetting situation. Those little experiences at the zoo turned out to be important mental healing points.

It was a great advantage that my friends had health care backgrounds. I had more than enough people to fuss over my wound care. Both Rita and Marilyn got carried away with cleaning my head. They are *really* into wound care.

The graft was maturing; in the process, there were a lot of scabs and loose skin tissue to be picked off. Like two birds sitting on the back of water buffalo on the African savanna, Rita and Marilyn took turns picking dead tissue from my head.

I actually credit them with a beautiful end result of the medical work of art that sits on top of my head. They certainly did not do the big installation job, but they did all the refinements and finishing touches that make it pleasing to the eye.

Jack

One of the best things that happened during my time at home was the arrival of Jack, our Rat Terrier puppy. Prior to our trip I had picked him out of a litter available from one of my bird friends.

Jack was born in June of 2005. Because I had rats bothering my birds, I thought a rat terrier would be a great dog to have. I would pick up Jack after our trip to Glacier. Yet now, I thought, the situation had obviously changed dramatically. How could I take care of a puppy while in a halo? My friend came to visit me with Jack and he was so small and timid that I thought he would actually be easy to deal with. Marilyn also thought it would be a welcome distraction. So one month after being home from the grizzly ordeal, our friend decided to donate the puppy to us.

Unfortunately, a couple of weeks after Jack came home, he broke his front leg while trying to get out of a playpen. So our "free" puppy now had to go to the vet for a potentially expensive procedure.

Marilyn and I stood at the veterinarian as he delivered the diagnosis and estimate. Little Jack had a serious fracture that would require surgery—$1,600 worth, in fact.

My Dutch brain immediately went into practical mode, and I started to think aloud. "Maybe this is too expensive and we should put him down?"

It took less than a split second for Marilyn to snap her head around to face me with an expression that instantaneously conveyed, "I can't believe you just said that."

"We didn't put you down, did we?" she asked.

Then she turned to the veterinarian.

"Of course we will do the surgery."

Man, did I feel sheepish and stupid.

Here I was, worried about money, while just two months earlier I had realized that money and earthly possessions mean nothing and that friends mean more than anything. Yet I'd been ready to put "man's best friend" down because fixing him would be too expensive.

Funny how life just keeps on reinforcing lessons like that.

The surgery was successful. A few days later we had Jack back home, wearing an Elizabethan collar around his head so he wouldn't chew on his cast. What a pair! Jack with his collar and cast, and me in my halo. He was like my mini-mascot. Jack's been my best buddy ever since.

CHAPTER 10

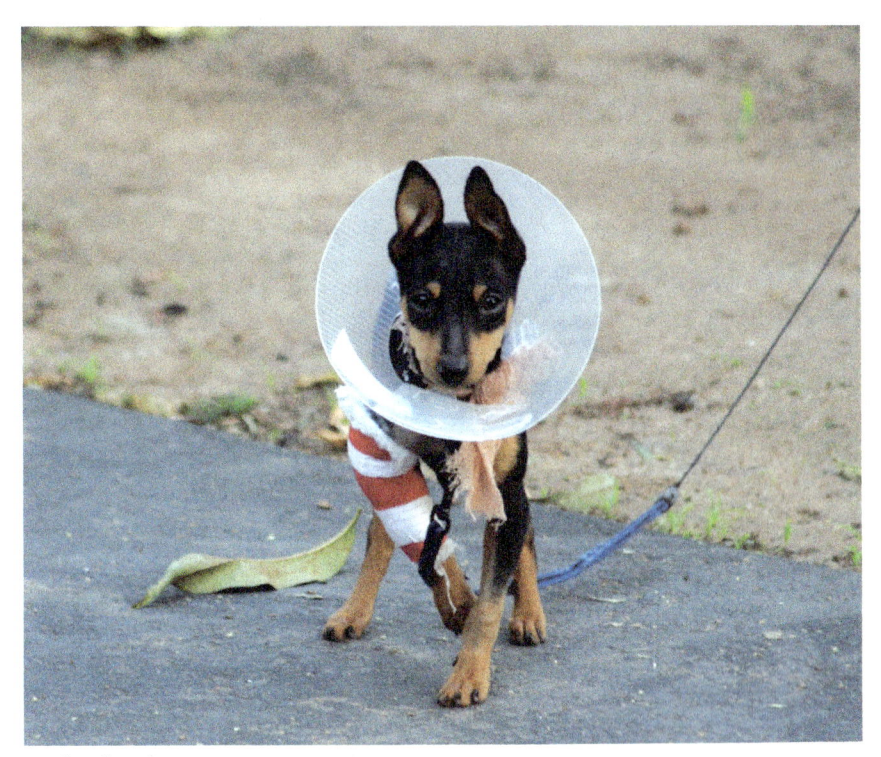

Jack after his surgery

Losing My Halo, Facing My Fear

From the minute the halo device had been screwed into my skull, I had been counting down the days until I would get it removed.

Of course, I had specifically requested the halo rather than spinal fusion surgery, but "be careful what you wish for."

When people asked me (and many did), "How is it having a halo?" I would answer, "It's like having a bird cage on your head." I would also tell them it was as uncomfortable as it looked. Indeed, I had to take a pain pill and a Valium first thing every morning. Sleeping was only possible on my back, and for a stomach-sleeper that was a trial to get used to, as well. (In the beginning I had to take a sleeping pill in addition to a Valium and a pain pill to get to sleep, but in time I was able to cut back.)

The halo slowly became more and more a part of my normal life. Although it was still miserable, I was able to walk quite well with it, and I was even able to drive with it.

Drive?

Yes.

We all have our challenges, and through the years, Marilyn's has become freeway driving. No matter how much she may want or even need to drive on a freeway to get from Point *A* to Point *B*, she gets panicky. It's not possible to get from our home in Escondido to San Diego without at least a little bit of freeway driving, but all those lanes of fast-moving traffic, aggressive drivers, and lane-splitting motorcyclists are just too much for her. Some people can't get on escalators; others can't walk within one hundred feet of the edge of a high cliff; Marilyn cannot drive on freeways.

So anytime I needed to go to a doctor's appointment and some freeway driving was involved, we would drive as far as we could without actually getting on the freeway, then we'd pull over and switch seats, and with the halo on, I would drive the one or two exits required to get back to local roads and side streets again.

When we did this, Marilyn had to be my eyes, of course. I certainly couldn't look over my shoulders with a metal ring screwed into my head. Thinking about what the whole "team driving" process must have looked like used to crack us up.

The day I went in to get the halo off was wonderful and scary at the same time. *What if I can't keep my head up anymore? What if my neck fracture did not heal well enough?* Luckily, my worries were unwarranted. It was liberating to finally get that thing screwed out of my head. There was even a photographer at the doctor's office ready to document the event.

CHAPTER 10 115

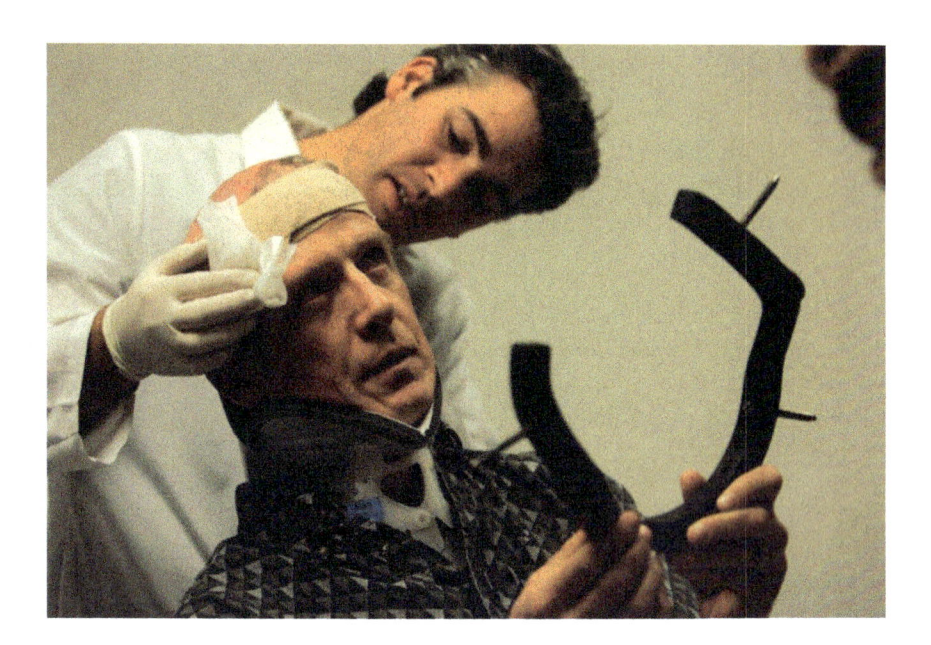

When X-rays were taken of my neck after the halo was removed, it looked as if I was physically ready for life without the bird cage around my head.

I also assumed that I was now ready to stop all my medications.

Unfortunately, the combination of removing my "protection" and stopping medications was not a wise move. Suddenly, I was without obvious markers that showed I had had a serious injury. The attack had, after all, happened only a couple months ago, and now I felt vulnerable and extremely fearful.

I realized I was unnerved when people walked past me. What if they bumped into me and dislodged something in my neck? I had enjoyed great personal space with the halo on; everyone stayed at least two to three feet away from me, or walked around me. But now I was back to the normal bumps, jostles and incidental contact of walking in the city. I definitely felt the invasion into what had been "my" space.

Without the halo, I also finally started to experience all the fear that I should have felt during this attack. The fear manifested itself primarily as crying jags that would come on for no apparent reason. Marilyn, who had been there at my side all along, became my rock at this time, and she helped me get through this period of displaced panic.

I should have been afraid of the bear; I should have been afraid to fall; I should have been afraid of dying; I should have been afraid that Jenna could have died. During these episodes, those fears and more kept looping around and around in my brain.

Eventually I called my boss, Mary Jo, who was an RN and let her know what was going on. She told me to get back on my medications. She said that I'd stopped too abruptly and should have been taken off gradually ("weaning protocol").

To MJ's credit, starting my anti-anxiety and pain medications again did take the edge of my fear away. Slowly but surely I was able to manage my fears much better. They returned at times when I was alone with my thoughts while running, and I cried many times, but every time I would just keep running and let them all play out to their logical end—in my mind, whatever I was fearful of became an event that had already happened to me and was now done.

I still experience these episodes of post-traumatic fear, although much less frequently. I figure these fear episodes are nature's way of helping my body and mind deal with all that had happened to me in smaller doses. Instead of pouring out the terror in one big deluge, they emerged in a time-delayed trickle when I was more physically able to cope with them.

Getting off all the medications was a slow process as well. I never actually did seek out any medical advice about how to wean off of them, so I just started to cut pills in half. After a week of half-pills, I went down to a quarter; after that, I figured it was safe to reduce that to nothing.

I don't think that was the most medically sound way to do things, but it worked.

I was also motivated because I had recently heard a story on NPR about pain medication addiction. That scared me into stopping as soon as possible.

After six months, I was finally done with Valium and Percocet.

— CHAPTER 11 —
The New Normal

My first post-attack Boston Marathon

During my recovery, running in a halo was obviously not possible, but when the device came off, I figured I had to start training again.

I have this love–hate relationship with running. Essentially, I hate getting up in the early morning (usually before 3 a.m.) and going out when it's cold and dark outside, but the moment I hit my stride, I feel the love.

My route is such a routine that I seem to do it in my sleep. I like to run by myself. Sometimes I get mired so deep in thought that I probably go no faster than ten to eleven minutes per mile. Occasionally, I forget where I have just been.

On long-run days, I actually get up before 2 a.m. (so maybe I'm actually asleep while I run). I admit I am pathological about it. To make sure I get up in time to do my long runs, I "trick" myself by setting the alarm for 3 a.m. on an alarm clock I've set ahead more than ninety minutes.

Stubborn.

In regard to my early morning running routine, people often ask me, "How do you do that?" My answer is, "I just do."

I was never much of an athlete in school, but running has given me a long-awaited sense of physical pride. It makes me feel accomplished—even a bit "macho"—to do something with my body most other people can't. I make a game of it too; I try to spot nighttime wildlife and keep a mental list of what I see. Rabbits are a common sight, but what I really look for are coyotes, raccoons, skunks, possums, owls, bats and the occasional deer. Once, while running at night, I even saw a bobcat. I nearly ran into it, creating an instant flashback to my bear attack event.

My goal is to spot specific animals every year. Crazy games like that can keep your mind busy while running up to twenty miles at once, training for a marathon.

The feeling that I get after running is awesome as well. Of course, it's also good for your health, assuming you don't fall.

Getting Back to Training

As much as I enjoy running, the first run after the attack was no fun at all.

I hated every step I took on that run. I was only able to run for ten to fifteen minutes. I did stick with it, obviously. Over the next couple of months I trained enough that I could do a marathon again. Working up to doing long runs lasting three to four hours was tough on the body, but good for the mind.

Adding some hill training was important as well; for several months I felt like a novice runner again, trying to prepare my body to endure 26.2 miles of pounding on the streets of San Diego.

I have run every Rock 'n' Roll Marathon in San Diego since the very first one. Grizzly bear or no, I wanted to keep that record intact. *Stubborn.* So on the first Sunday in June, 2006, within ten months of the encounter at Glacier, I was at it again.

I was not happy with my time at all.

A 3:39 marathon? That was more than ten minutes slower than the year before! Yet I had trained so well! I had done the track, the tempo work and the interval training, in addition to the many long runs. I even had a bicyclist with me for most of the marathon to keep me on pace.

So why was I unhappy with my time? I should have been happy that I could walk at all, let alone run a marathon, but something interesting happens when you lose physical ability. You reset your goals based on what you think is physically possible.

In my case, I figured, I really did not have any good reason not to be back to normal again. True, I had lost a muscle from my side that now was sitting on top of my head. And I could not see down with my right eye. And sure, there'd been surgeries, and some other minor stuff, but that was nothing. Heck, there are people who complete marathons in wheelchairs!

Back to the training schedule again.

I had to train harder or differently to regain my sub-3:30 time and qualify for Boston.

The following year, when I did my second marathon after the attack, I improved my time by five minutes. Woohoo!

I was on the right track. Now my PBPR (post-bear personal record) was at 3:35. Just five minutes to shave off in order to qualify for the Boston marathon in my age group.

The grizzly bear had been such a dominant force in my life the last twenty-two months; I wanted to take strength and experience from this accident and finally move it into the positive column.

With sheer willpower (some may call it *stubbornness*), perseverance and a coach paid for by the Los Angeles Marathon folks, I did eventually get below a 3:30 marathon time.

Yes, a coach from the Los Angeles Marathon.

It turned out the organizers of that event had read my story in the *Los Angeles Times* and gave me the Patsy Choco Courage award for what I had done to save my daughter's life. It was totally unexpected. To help me get back to normal, they contacted a local coach who would work with me to get fast enough to qualify for Boston again. After about three years, Marilyn and I traveled to St. George, Utah, where I ran a marathon, and I came in at 3:28—exhausted, hurting on the outside, but ecstatic on the inside.

My successful finish was due in part to a cute, petite blond young woman who started cussing at me, loudly and unexpectedly, about a mile from the finish line when I thought I couldn't run anymore. She shocked me back into running; the language and the look just didn't match. I have no idea who she was, but she made me keep running—and pushing to the finish.

A lot of healing occurred with that marathon. A three-year journey was successfully completed.

In the following years, I completed more and more marathons. In 2013, back in St. George, I reset my PBPR and ran a 3:25.

One at a time, memories would come back over the next few years during my runs. It was as if every once in a while, nature decided that I could handle another punch. Here it is; take it, deal with it, comprehend it and get on with it. My running was like therapy: I had a session every morning, and then, once a week or once a month, a breakthrough.

Realizations, such as how far Jenna had fallen would suddenly hit me and I would start crying while running. Realizing that my head had been bitten by a grizzly bear would suddenly rise to real consciousness; it was as though I'd heard the words before, but didn't really accept it until that moment.

As I ran, my mind played out every detail related to the attack, picture by picture, an interior slide show—only this slide show had been going for years now.

Just when I'd think the slide show was finished, a new realization would come. Then the show would start over.

I think this intermittent sequence of memories will last the rest of my life.

Media and Presentations

There are news people, and then there are tabloid news people. In any profession there are the good and the bad, and I certainly found that out.

My story had become national news, and over the next few years everyone wanted a piece of it. I never received any sort of monetary payment to discuss the event, but Jenna and I did some awesome travel: Toronto, New York, Yellowstone, and locally in the San Diego and Los Angeles area.

The first media exposure had been the early Seattle press conference, and as Gary Moses had predicted, I would be getting media requests for the next three to five years. Even now, more than ten years later, I still get the occasional request to be interviewed. The most recent request was for a limited ABC series called *In an Instant*, featuring a two-hour long re-enactment of the events that took place when

Jenna and I were attacked. It was interspersed with interviews from me, Jenna, and other key people in our story.

I am sure the media used our story to draw an audience, but I used the media just as much, because for me, sharing the experience was like therapy. After every interview I felt a little bit better. I've cried many times in front of the camera (and still do) because the minute I start to talk about how much people have done for me, I get very emotional.

At heart, I am a giver and not a taker, and so at times I still struggle with feeling I haven't deserved the help, friendship, and care of so many other people in the aftermath of the events at Glacier. Yet I am immensely thankful for everything. It is pretty awesome to see that strangers will come to your aid in your hour of need, while friends and acquaintances will go out of their way to see you have all that you need.

I can still see the crawl across the bottom of the TV screen to announce that Jenna and I would be interviewed next when we appeared on the *Today* show: "Hero father saves daughter in gruesome grizzly bear attack." I remember thinking, *"Hero? Of course not. I'm just a dad who did what every other dad would do in a situation where his child's life was in danger."* For a normal person like me to be called a hero on national TV…well, that is unbelievable.

My best media experience was with the *Los Angeles Times* (*LA Times*), and specifically Tom Curwen, the writer who covered my story, and photographer Al Schaben. Tom and I met by chance at Scripps Memorial Hospital where I was being treated. He had seen me walking with my therapist one day, and he asked the nurses if I was that guy who had been attacked.

He felt he wanted to know a little bit more about my case. He interviewed and got to know both me and Jenna. That "little bit" turned in to a feature story divided into two parts. For his efforts, Tom became a finalist for the Pulitzer Prize that year.

Tom traveled with us to Glacier twice; the first time for the first big story, and the second time a few years later for a follow-up article. Al Schaben came along as well. Neither gentleman had been to Glacier before; Al was pretty scared and nervous we'd run into a bear. (Very understandable—he'd seen all my mauling pictures and he was a dad with a very young family.)

On the day we hiked the Grinnell Glacier Trail, Gary Moses was with us. He instructed us to clap our hands and yodel along the way, especially when we could not see twenty-five feet or less around us in any direction. This was the best way to warn wildlife we were on the trail.

Al tended to clap a lot, regardless of how well we could see our path, and that amused Gary. I liked it because it was one more noise machine that would send warning signals out.

Walking with the LA Times *crew up the Grinnell Glacier Trail again.*

The comments after the *LA Times* story broke were all positive.

Other media moments came at strange times. Lisa Ohmstede, the public relations manager for the hospital where I worked, became my pseudo-agent. (I promised her half the proceeds from all the exposure, and so far I have kept my part of the bargain, because she has received 50 percent of nothing.) Lisa traveled with us as needed;

in fact, she got to go with us to the *Today* show. The day after the *LA Times* ran the story in the Sunday edition, the phones went crazy. All the major networks wanted to have Jenna and me on the next day. Of course, all these networks are located in New York, which meant we had to hop on a plane. Lisa was the one handling all the arrangements, and we were thankful.

Once in New York, Jenna and I stayed in a little hotel suite near Rockefeller Center so we could walk to the *Today* show taping the next day. As we were being prepared for our TV interview, we felt vaguely as if we were part of a freak show. Naturally we understood people were interested in survival stories, but it is an odd thing to be recognized for nearly dying.

While waiting in the green room, both Jenna and I felt like saying to others sitting there, "So, what are you in for?" and "What kind of a freak are you?"

Part of that stemmed from activity in the makeup department. The makeup artists were very nice, but it seemed fairly obvious that they wanted to enhance our scars, or at least make sure that they were visible for the TV audience. Jenna actually said something like, "Why don't you color that in a bit," as one of the women worked near her facial scar. (I'm still not sure if the makeup artists caught that.)

The live taping process itself is also fun, especially if the person asking you questions has barely any understanding what has happened to you. I always had one or two messages in mind that I wanted to make sure to focus on; usually it was the importance of trauma systems and/or one tip on how to stay safe while hiking in grizzly country. I also always tried to say something nice about the *LA Times*, Scripps Health, and everyone who had helped me. TV appearances are kind of nerve-wracking though, because I never want to convey something that I did not intend to say. When I am with Jenna, it all goes very smoothly; she is quite articulate.

The end product of these tapings looks good most of the time, yet occasionally I wonder if we ever did a disservice to the public by offering only a superficial look at the facts. Because two minutes is about all the time TV interviewers have with you. Then they are rushed by their producers to get to the next story.

While TV talk shows may only allow for short interviews, adventure documentary shows are a different "animal." These types of shows want in-depth information. Sometimes these shows tend to glom onto the worst aspects of a situation, rather than searching for teachable moments. Yes, our attack was quite gruesome—but that part lasted only about ten to fifteen minutes. The rest of the day doesn't make as exciting a story, but within that timeframe are all the reasons why we eventually survived the ordeal. Adventure shows usually focus on the former, to the detriment of the latter.

To me, the gift of a second life demands that I share what I've learned. I do so, in part, by speaking publicly about what happened to Jenna and myself.

I have spoken at trade shows for manufacturers of halos, impressing on them the importance of telling the patient what to expect. I have spoken for healthcare audiences, expressing to them how to make the medical experience less stressful for patients without spending more, and possibly even spending less. I have spoken in classrooms and professional meetings with audience sizes ranging from barely a dozen to nearly 500. I have also spoken for many TV audiences where the interviewer and the camera people become my muses. If their reactions to my story are similar to the reactions I get from larger audiences, then I know I am effectively getting my points across. Luckily, I have always had that same experience with a small group as I had for a larger crowd. One time, I even had an interviewer run in to the production booth to tell the producer he needed more time to talk to me. He proceeded to take an extra four minutes, which is an eternity in TV land.

Each time I give my bear presentation, I wonder if I will be able to keep the audience engaged for the next hour. Within minutes, though, the audience gets very quiet. No one checks their phone or watch, and they all stare. Maybe they sense that this is something that could happen to anyone—even one of them. The attack story seems to release something that is very much still part of our subconscious: the fear of the beast in the forest that comes out from behind a bush.

Of course, nowadays, most of us do not hunt for our food, but I can imagine that a few hundred years ago, when humans did not live in such an industrialized world, that a wild animal attack could be a reality. These days, danger comes more from fellow humans than from wild animals.

Still, Jenna and I did experience this primal danger firsthand, and through that, we seem to connect with people in a way that releases deeply buried memories of terrible events that have happened to them.

Indeed, we should not have survived this ordeal. But since we did, our story seems to give hope to others that they, too, can survive their ordeals. And occasionally, I've had somebody tell me after a presentation, "Your story renews my faith in humankind."

Mine, too.

— CHAPTER 12 —
Return to Glacier

Less than one year from the date of our accident, we returned to Montana. Jenna, Marilyn, and I were invited to attend the annual A.L.E.R.T. fundraiser in April of 2006 (Stephanie was in school and stayed home).

This would be our first time back to Montana. We'd hazily formed half-thoughts about going to Glacier anyway, as I had made an "appointment" with Gary Moses to come by and thank him for all he had done. He was one of my heroes, and I knew I wanted to eventually go back, say hello to him, and bring him a thank-you note from Jenna and myself.

The day we arrived in Kalispell it was rainy. We took our rental car to Glacier to visit Gary, but we arrived a bit too early, so we drove up the Going to the Sun Road until we could go no further.

Our stop was an area called Avalanche Lake. All three of us got out of the car; Jenna was visibly afraid and jumpy. Later Marilyn told me that Jenna had nearly jumped out of her skin when they heard a sound of crackling among the bushes as they walked a few feet over to the restroom. Unlike Jenna, I had a strange sense of total calm and peace; no fear whatsoever.

When we drove back down and eventually got to Gary's office I recognized him, but he certainly did not recognize me. Knowing now how I looked at the time of the attack, I can certainly understand that.

Gary was visibly moved that we had come to thank him. Jenna and I had composed a thank-you note and added a picture that we framed.

To: Glacier National Park Forest Rangers

Date: April 29, 2006

Thank you for all that you did for us on August 25, 2005. We would not be alive without your expertise and care. When we were suddenly attacked by a mother grizzly bear, we did not know if we would survive. With a lot of luck we miraculously escaped alive.

We were so happy to see you when you came to our side after fellow hikers had found us. The medical care that you were able to provide to us on the mountain saved our lives. We were so impressed by your expertise, calm, personable attitude and persistence. I still vividly remember Gary Moses saying, "You hear that sound? That is the sound of your rescue" when the first helicopter came by. Unbeknownst to us, a large group of park personnel was working on alternative options to get us to safety. We are so grateful for all your efforts that day. Hanging on a rope under a helicopter was definitely not part of our vacation plan but with your guidance it all went picture perfect.

Your efforts and your caring touched us deeply and you will always have a special place in our hearts.

Thank you for saving our lives,

Jenna and Johan Otter

The four of us—Marilyn, Jenna, Gary, and I—talked about the attack and how people reacted to it back at the ranger station.

Then Gary asked us if we wanted to take a ride up the Going-to-the-Sun Road, past the point where the road was blocked. Of course we wanted that! What a treat to get to ride with a ranger beyond the no-admittance zone.

Gary drove us up all the way beyond the loop, until a recent rockslide blocked our way. On the way up, Gary explained the difference between Hemlock and Cedar, and he pointed out some Harlequin ducks in the stream. Once we were at the highest point, he pointed out the snowfield on Angels Peak. That field comes crashing down every spring once the snow has melted to a point that it does not stick to the mountainside anymore. We saw snow geese flying high overhead, and far above us on the rocky crags, a mountain goat watched us.

Jenna and I got to take a picture with Gary. I look like a dope—but that was because I was so in awe of him and what we were allowed to see that day.

After spending the morning with Gary, we went to visit the Reindls, who had invited us to dinner. Heidi Reindl was one of the two young women who had helped to save us, and her mother had looked out for Jenna while she was in the hospital. They made us a great dinner. We will never forget watching the busy beavers (literally!) in the pond right in front of their house. Now we know why they call them busy beavers—they never stopped moving and we would have loved to never stop watching them.

Phil and Jeanette Reindl with us in front of their "beaver pond"

The next evening, as we dressed for the fundraising dinner, I was a bit nervous. I did not know if I should wear a cap or not. Until that point I had been rather leery about showing my head, afraid people would make fun of it or stare at it. This night, Marilyn told me that my head looked fine without the cap, so for the first time ever, I went out in public without a head cover. The feeling was absolutely uncanny; I felt naked. When we got out of the car and walked to the horse arena where the event was to be held, I was nervous about what peoples' reactions would be, but no one stared or asked about my bald head. Instead, they were hospitable and happy to see us. One of the young physicians who had helped me in the emergency room in August came to me and told me that I had been the most thankful patient ever.

CHAPTER 12

Dr. Iwersen, Jenna and me at the A.L.E.R.T. banquet

The organizers of the event had asked me if I would say the evening prayer for the audience. I felt I had to say yes, even though I am not that religious.

I had grown up with parents that were quite skeptical about organized religion. We always prayed before meals and believed in God, but my dad and mom had seen too many bad things happen by so-called "very religious people"—things that were in direct opposition to what Jesus had taught, according to the Bible. We therefore did not belong to any religious organization or church, but had gone to a Christian school from high school on.

And yet, the people in Montana had been so nice, honest, and comforting, I suddenly had no problem at all saying a prayer:

"Thank you, God, for giving me the opportunity to give this blessing for these individuals you brought to our rescue. Thank you for the hikers, the rangers, the rescue workers, the hospital workers, and our friends and family. Without all their help, we would not be standing here. Please bless and encourage all these people. I talked a lot to you that day on the mountain and you showed your kindness through all these incredible people. Words cannot express how blessed we are to be in your daily presence. I am asking for your blessing so these people can continue their work and I ask you to give them strength, courage, and wisdom. We pray for your guidance as other individuals come across our path. It has been said that the one who takes your hand and touches your heart is a true friend. Many of these people here are my true friends. Please guide their hands to reach and touch many more lives.

In God's name, Amen."

The Annual Glacier National Park Hike

After they hear about our story, people ask me if I ever go back to Glacier National Park.

I tell them that I went back to hike ten months after the attack.

I felt I had to finish the trail and see if the end destination was actually worth all this.

Well, the trail's endpoint was even more beautiful than I thought it was going to be. Since then I have gone back to Glacier every year, and I will continue to make this annual trip for the foreseeable future.

My sense of feeling at home has continued since that first time we were back in the park. In 2006, we finished the Grinnell Glacier hike with people from the *LA Times*. Gary Moses led the way.

I wanted to see where the bear attack had happened, but Jenna was not yet ready to revisit it. She opted to stay at school and continue with her dance studies. Marilyn did come along with me. It was truly an amazing hike. I know "amazing" is an overused word, but nothing describes the trail better, especially given my motivation for being on it.

It was a beautiful July day, and we made lots of noise as we hiked. Gary was able to show us where the attack had occurred—from the spot on the trail where we first saw the grizzly, to the ledge where I ultimately landed.

We were actually able to get onto the ledge upon which I'd fallen, but we did a rather stupid thing. Marilyn opted not to hike down the embankment to the ledge, and she stayed on the trail. But the moment after we disappeared from her view, she realized that she was now alone on the trail without bear spray. (I thought by now we should have known better than to leave somebody by herself in bear country without bear spray!)

Seeing the landscape of the mountain in a relaxed state of mind made me realize how incredibly lucky we had been. The ledge was much smaller in width than I had thought it was, and the mountain was much steeper than what I remembered. I was astonished our fellow hikers had even been able to get down to us. They had risked their own lives—or at least the danger of an injury.

Another exciting thing happened on that first trip back. After Marilyn and I checked into our hotel the first day, we decided to take our rental car over to Logan Pass. As usual, we were not disappointed with the beautiful views and the serenity of the place. I was hanging back, taking pictures, (with a new camera the rehab staff at the hospital had bought for me) when suddenly I heard someone call, "Johan!" I remember thinking, "OK, who knows me here?"

It was Ken Justus, the A.L.E.R.T. helicopter pilot, who had just spent the day climbing one of the peaks in the park with his buddy, and he'd recognized me. We talked a bit, and I invited him to come hiking with me in two days, when I would be meeting some folks who were making a short film about a grizzly DNA study that was currently being conducted. It would be nice to have company; Marilyn was not interested in going. Ken said he'd check his schedule, but he never did get back to me.

I was surprised, then, to see Ken on the day I met with the film folks. The crew filmed me while we looked out on the Many Glaciers Valley. We had decided to hike the Swift Current Pass from Many Glaciers all the way to Logan Pass.

From the hike with Gary and the LA Times team, I had learned how to yodel and clap my hands at appropriate intervals to avoid bears. I was loud, but I did not care, nor did the rest of our party. When we got to the top of the pass, we spotted a wolverine! Even with being as loud as we were, we still spotted one of the more elusive creatures of the park. Awesome!

During the hike, Ken told me that I should come back after Labor Day, when most of the tourists are gone. He also said that the fall colors are spectacular at Glacier, and that some of the pine trees, called Larches, turn golden and lose their needles. I promised him I would think about it.

What started out as a suggestion from Ken has turned into an annual pilgrimage to Glacier. Ken and I have become great friends, and every year I go on my hiking "mancation" with him.

Jenna has come with me several times, as have friends and relatives. Who needs a man cave when you can have an entire national park?

Ken and I have done many trails and hiked in every kind of weather, from hurricane-like windstorms to crisp autumn days. One time Jenna, Ken, and I tried to protect ourselves from strong winds by squatting under some one-foot-tall juniper bushes. Didn't work too well, but better than nothing. We've fished most of the fish-worthy lakes in the park and have even done back-country camping. I once swore I would never just want a thin layer of nylon tent between me and a potential bear, but the first time I camped at Glacier, I had the best sleep ever.

My great friend and pilot Ken and me enjoying a "barley pop" after finishing the Two-Bear Marathon in Whitefish, MT

I love when Jenna is with Ken and me—she is the most sensible person in the party. Ken has no fear whatsoever, and true to form, I am always engrossed in nature to the point of ignoring everything else. So just Ken and I together are not the best or safest pair. Jenna adds some common sense to the mix and she is also a fantastic hiker—probably better than either one of us.

One time we went out as a trio, we did see a grizzly bear while hiking. We were in the Two Medicine area. Ken spotted it about two miles away, very far away from where we were heading.

Jenna on the way to Iceberg Lake, her first hike two years after the attack and concurring Siyeh Pass a few years later

— POSTSCRIPT —

What can I say? The T-shirt says it all.

Do miracles exist? Is it luck or sheer coincidence that some of us survive terrible events while others do not? I do not have the answers to these questions, nor does anyone else, yet I see a miracle every time I look in the mirror or when I see my daughter, Jenna.

On August 25, 2005, my life changed in a fraction of a second—somewhere between 0.2 and 0.7 seconds. That amount of time doesn't really exist in my conscious life, but it was the time I needed to step between life and death.

Having my daughter with me did not allow me to drift off. I had to concentrate and think better and faster than I ever had in my life.

I now recognize how insignificant my own life is to me in comparison to the life of my children. Death would not be painful or horrible, as long as my children were safe.

I also wanted to stay alive for Marilyn. She is my hero and best friend. I am very blessed to have her as my spouse and will forever be overwhelmingly in her debt for giving me two beautiful daughters and for all the humor, arguments, and laughter we share.

Marilyn and me next to the rock on the trail where Jenna first spotted the bear and where I stood my ground

Since the attack at Glacier, I have found greater meaning in the notion that we live our lives for our families and loved ones. This concept—keeping loved ones safe—seems to resonate deeply for a lot of people when I give my bear story presentations, especially for parents. We all say that we would give our lives for our children, but many of us have never had to do that, so we don't really know. If pushed, we hope we would react in protective mode.

Interestingly, I've sometimes had people react with envy when they hear my story, because (unlike them) I know that I will give my life for my child, without question. More importantly, both of my children know that their dad would give his life for them, and there is no greater gift I can give them than that.

After an attack as severe as ours, the memories remain for a lifetime. If you allow them to be, they could be painful and all-consuming. I've tried to find ways to channel them in positive ways. Maybe it's just in my nature to be optimistic.

Way back in Seattle, in the immediate aftermath of the attack, Marilyn made a very astute observation: "Every time the doctors or nurses come to tell you something, it's always good news. You have not had bad news yet, and if you did, you'd be able to somehow turn it into good news anyway." I have turned her comment into one of my mantras: when things don't go as I plan, I make the best of it. So, Jenna has a scar on her face, but it is not disfiguring—she is still as beautiful as ever; in fact, the scar adds character. My unexpectedly hairless head has been much easier to deal with than actually going bald gradually. I consider it a medical work of art with a great story attached to it; plus I save a lot of money by not having to go to the hairdresser anymore, and I never have a bad hair day.

As a result of this event, I've been rewarded with renewed family relationships and new friendships. I re-established a great relationship with long-lost cousins with whom I had not been in contact for years. I also made some great new friends. I have visited places that I had never visited before—Toronto, Niagara Falls, the island of Lanai, and of course, Seattle.

My relationship with Jenna is deeper than it was before the accident. We share a special bond due to our incredibly intense experience—an experience that we would not wish upon anyone else, but now that we have had it, I wouldn't want to part with that. It is a part of the past that was able to bring something out of me I did not know I had.

Throughout the first three years of recovery, I wish I could have shut up more about this bear thing. I would bring it up continuously, and Jenna would endure it, although at times she'd ask me to please stop talking about it. I needed the outlet to unload my feelings, and no one but Jenna knew what this actually was like.

My favorite "bear claw"—one filled with huckleberry from the Polebridge Mercantile with my foot for size comparison

Time and time again I have had people come up to me after my talk, tears in their eyes as they thank me for telling my story. All these folks share a common theme, which is that our story released some hidden emotion they had not completely dealt with. Seeing me so openly talk about my own struggles to deal with trauma seems to reassure them that they are okay; they can let go of their nagging feeling that they should be healed by now.

It turns out a lot of people have unrealistic expectations of how fast they should be able to physically and emotionally heal from traumatic experiences. The truth is that some of us are never healed and sometimes it takes a lifetime. And that's OK.

People are also drawn to our story, I think, by their fear of fear itself. We shun situations in which we may experience fear because it suggests something bad may happen. Our attack was certainly a terrifying situation, yet during the attack itself, I did not experience any fear at all. It was as if there was no room in my brain for fear. I had to step outside of what was happening to me so that I could protect Jenna.

Decisions had to be made quickly and sequentially: Should we jump? Should I pull the bear with me? One after the other, no decision was really that hard to make; the situation was very much black and white. Afterward, I was proud of how methodical I'd been, and I was stoked to realize that I could make so many potentially life-and-death decisions in such a short time, all leading to life.

When I experienced the out-of-body sensation during the attack, I thought it was not very helpful, and I was happy that I "came back in" and went back to the decision-making that had saved my life up until that point. Looking back, I realize that out-of-body moments are needed for survival. Being killed by an animal, it turns out, doesn't hurt at all. There is no pain, no fear; it's just something that happens and it is done. Our body seems to have a mechanism to help us through the part right before death.

I could (and still can) easily imagine that in that Hollywood movie I imagined myself in very briefly, the lights could have suddenly switched off. And that would have been it. My life would have been over. Very matter-of-fact.

I am also sure that, had I been killed, news headlines would have said something like "Father dies gruesomely trying to protect his daughter," and my family and friends would have all thought what a horrible death it must have been—but in reality it wouldn't have been.

The whole ordeal has certainly left me with a decreased fear of death, but no closer to knowing if there really is a heaven. ("It must be good, because no one has ever come back from it," as my father used to say.)

My physical scars do not bother me one bit. In fact, I am proud of them. Hardly ever does anyone ask what happened to my head, and when people do ask, they are so shocked and awed by the reason, they sometimes tell me I have a beautiful head. I agree. (I am, I realize, very lucky that my injuries did not affect my appearance, other than premature 100 percent baldness. If that had been the case, I am sure I would not be so lighthearted about my scars.)

Today, I live life to its fullest. I am running several marathons each year. After the attack, I earned my doctorate degree in Physical Therapy. I became a senior member of the administrative team at

Scripps Health in San Diego, where I am responsible for the health and safety of nearly 15,000 employees. I breed my birds and grow my fruit. In fact, I enjoy life so much and so intensely that I feel I am living my second life.

One of my daughters' favorite films when they were growing up was *Strictly Ballroom*. A line in that movie that has always stuck with me; "A life lived in fear is a life half lived." I live my life by that motto as well, and am never afraid to start a new adventure (although it has to be reasonable; I'll skip skydiving because I see no reason to pay for jumping out of a perfectly well-functioning plane).

Let life happen. Enjoy it. Discover one new thing every day. Share your story. Help others to be able to share their stories as well. Stories can make the world a better place. Bad things will happen. You cannot and must not succumb to that.

Be *stubborn*.

May you also live your life twice—and well.

If you survive an attack by a grizzly bear, you become...

"One with the spirit of the grizzly"
— Native American Lore

Our family at Jenna's graduation from Columbia Medical School

— ACKNOWLEDGMENTS —

Here I thank all the people I didn't thank by name in the book itself. I thank everybody I have ever wanted to thank. I thank the people who told me to write a book. I thank the people who read early drafts or bits and pieces. I thank people who contributed their own recollections. I thank the schoolkids who were so happy we were OK after they read the story but still had to ask if I had survived. I thank all the medical professionals in the world who collectively improved medicine so Jenna and I could survive and thrive. I thank the growers of blackberries in Washington State, because you provided me my first best meal after the attack. I thank God. I thank all lovers of nature and protectors of the environment. I thank the whole wide world and especially all my friends and family—with friends and family everything is possible.

The end of the Grinnell trail and of this book. Thank you for reading.

Johan